FOUND
OF T
NATIONAL
TRUST

FOUNDERS OF THE NATIONAL TRUST

GRAHAM MURPHY

New edition published in Great Britain in
2002 by National Trust Enterprises Ltd

First published in 1987 by Christopher Helm
(Publishers) Ltd

Original text © 1987 Graham Murphy

New edition © 2002 Graham Murphy

Japanese translation byProfessor Tadahiro Yotsumoto,
The English Agency (Japan) Ltd. 1992.

British Library Cataloguing in Publication Data

Murphy, Graham
    Founders of the National Trust: a study
    of Sir Robert Hunter, Octavia Hill and
    Canon Rawnsley.
    1. National Trust—Biography
    I. Title
    719'.068042   NX28.G72N37

ISBN 0–7078–0332–2

Printed in Great Britain by
Creative Print and Design, Ebbw Vale, Wales

Contents

Illustrations

Between pages 96 and 97

Preface

The thought of writing something about the founders of the National Trust came to me on a September afternoon in Hawkshead, more years ago now than I care to remember, during my first Lake District holiday since a childhood Scout camp at Coniston. I was curious to know how a voluntary organisation which had acquired so much beautiful scenery had come into existence. At the local National Trust Information Centre there was a leaflet available explaining that the Trust was the offspring of the Commons Preservation Society. While in London, I visited the CPS in somewhat dingy offices in an old building in Seven Dials. There I was made welcome, given a desk and the freedom of their library. (The CPS has since moved to Henley-on-Thames and is now the Open Spaces Society.) Further research took me back to the Lake District, to which, like so many others, I have now become extremely attached.

Without the help of friends the completion of this book would have taken much longer, particularly Rosalind Rawnsley, who has worked closely with me for several months, revising, helping to clarify the text and typing the final draft; working with her has been a great encouragement and pleasure and I would like to thank her, and her husband John, for many days of hospitality at their home in Shropshire. My thanks also go to the Rev. Principal Tony Cross for the vacation-time peace of Harris Manchester College, Oxford, which helped along the writing.

There has been no history of the open space movement in the nineteenth century since the publication of Lord Eversley's *Commons, Forests and Footpaths* in 1910, and no library contains a really substantial collection of the books and copies of the manuscripts relevant to this subject. I am therefore indebted to many people in different parts of the country for assisting me: R. Allen, the Rev. John Allerton, David Anscombe, Beryl Brooks, John Chapman of the Forestry Commission, Howard Hull and Nina Atkinson of the Brantwood Trust, the Rev. Rodney Hughes, Ruth Hunter-Maunsell, the Rev. John Keggen, Bryan Matthews, David Maufe, Conrad Rawnsley, the Rev. John Roberts, Harry Ruckley, G.E. Simpson, David Steers, Jane Wates, the Rev. Eric Wild, all the staff of the Open Spaces Society and Elizabeth Battrick, Christopher Hanson-Smith, Lawrence Rich, Margaret Willes, Helen Fewster and Barbara Mercer of the National Trust. The staff of the following Libraries and Record Offices have been unfailingly helpful: Avon County Reference Library, Bristol; the British Library; City of Birmingham Library; Carlisle Records Office; Cumbria Records Office, Kendal; Guildhall Library; House of Lords Records Office; John Rylands Library, Manchester; Kendal Public Library; Keswick Museum; Liverpool Central Library; Marylebone Public Library; the National Trust Library; St Deiniol's Library, Hawarden; Surrey Records Office and the Wordsworth Museum, Grasmere.

PREFACE TO THE SECOND EDITION

Since 1987 when this book was first published, the history of the National Trust has become more widely known. Following the demise of the founders, the organisation gained the political momentum rightly accorded to it by Professor D. Cannadine in his biography of the historian G. M. Trevelyan (1992), chairman of the National Trust Estates Committee from 1928 to 1949. It was during the latter half of this period that Philip Kerr, 11th Marquess of Lothian, used his influence to initiate the process of acquiring for the Trust some of the finest of Britain's great houses. This scheme, under which landowners no longer able to afford their upkeep could offer them to the National Trust for preservation, or through which the Treasury would accept a worthy property in lieu of death duties and hand it over to the Trust for the nation, was entrusted to James Lees-Milne. Even allowing for some understandable hyperbole, Lees-Milne's published diaries highlight the extraordinary success of this initiative.

The present volume being concerned principally with the foundation and early years of the National Trust, it remains for other writers to document and evaluate its later history. With the passage of time perceptions of historical events are reinterpreted, and the roles and importance of different protagonists re-evaluated. This process has already become evident in the works of John Gaze (*Figures in a Landscape*, 1988) and Merlin Waterson (*The National Trust, The First Hundred Years*, 1994), both however writing from a perspective within the organisation. Paula Weideger (*Gilding the Acorn: Behind the Façade of the National Trust*, 1994), as an American, 'who voted in another country and for whom the class system had no place' and without an axe to grind, identified an opportunity for someone from outside to write about this 'very English institution'. Her breezy and questioning approach ruffled many feathers at the time.

What she described, in her account of the Extraordinary General Meeting called by Commander Conrad Rawnsley in 1967 when he was Appeals Director, as 'an old boy network', is a perception which is still held by some today. However, many of the reforms which Rawnsley advocated have since been implemented, and it could be argued that the National Trust has benefited in the long term from his raising of the tempest.

History, as a subjective discipline, never stands still, and the Trust as the national institution which it has become will no doubt be the subject of much future debate and reinterpretation when we of the present generation have also passed, like the founders, into history.

G.M. 2002

Introduction

On the afternoon of 16 October 1902, Brandlehow Park, on the shores of Derwentwater, the National Trust's first Lake District land holding, was declared open to the public by HRH Princess Louise. It was the first National Trust property to be opened by royalty. A mixture of pasture, oak woods and wetland, Brandlehow, with its claim to the rights of an adjacent fell common, is reached from Keswick by a footpath which had been kept open as the result of a heated dispute, fomented by one of the Trust's three founders. Protection of the countryside, the preservation of woodlands, rights of common and rights of way, had all been concerns of the Trust's founders for a long time before the birth of their joint organisation, and just how the Trust came to be conceived is intimately bound up with the story of their lives. The seeds were sown at the beginning of the open space movement, in which all three played an active part, and the flowering of the National Trust was their crowning achievement.

With over 612,000 acres of land, the National Trust is now the largest private landowner in the United Kingdom (excluding Scotland) with moorland, fells and fens, farms, woods, lakes and islands, villages, country houses and castles, parks and ornamental gardens and more than half of the finest coastline in England, Wales and Northern Ireland. The Trust does not aim simply to preserve land and buildings, but also to keep intact the whole social fabric of those parts of the countryside for which it is directly responsible. Its stately homes and historic houses are immensely popular, and the way of life of the landowning classes is what has most preoccupied the Trust in its presentation of the nation's history.

While maintaining the quality of life in the countryside takes up a major portion of its resources, the urban environment, and indeed the countryside not immediately under its protection are not normally seen as the Trust's concern. In this respect the policy of the National Trust appears not to be entirely that of its founders. Their involvement in the open space movement stemmed from a profound concern for the quality of life for people everywhere. Making no distinction between town and country, they saw freedom to enjoy unspoilt beauty and open skies as a universal right.

CHAPTER 1

The Beginning of the Open Space Movement

The greater part of the English countryside as we know it today
bears all the hallmarks of private property; fields curtained with
ditches and hedges, hills divided and encircled by walls, woodlands with fences. Only the high moors and mountains are largely
free of man-made barriers. Occasionally, however, in lowland
areas, there appears to our view a stretch of open land varying in
size from a few acres of village heath to perhaps several miles of
forest which in all its history has never felt the touch of a plough.
Seldom as uniformly green as the land of tillage and pure pasture,
these vestiges of primaeval wilderness wear subdued colours,
colours whose intensity, as described by Thomas Hardy, is 'more
usually reached by way of the solemn than by way of the brilliant'.[1]
Such are the 'common lands', a description that does not imply any
lack of ownership but rather that the right to graze stock, pick fruit,
take away wood, bracken, turf, peat, stone or sand would at one
time have belonged to those living in the immediate neighbourhood who were designated 'commoners'. Industry too once flour-
ished upon these islands of unkempt nature: the specialised skills
of the charcoal-burner, the clog-cutter and the rake-maker, the
bowl-turner and the chair-bodger. They followed the slow movement of the growth of woods like a primitive hunter dogging his
herd. They moved from place to place; living in a fragile hut, heat-
ing a temporary kiln, sitting under the open sky at a makeshift
bench or pole-lathe wherever the raw materials were to hand.

These primitive rural industries have long since vanished, and
today the grazing of animals is almost the only common right still
exercised. The survival of common lands owes more to human
indifference than to human interest in their exploitation. The

greater part of what remains has endured mainly because it was thought to be of poor agricultural value. Consequently it was not subject to any legal transition from communal to private usage before the second half of the nineteenth century, when a halt was called to the processes of wholesale enclosure by means of privately sponsored and officially encouraged Inclosure Acts. From 1700 until the 1873–4 land census, Parliament approved nearly 5,000 Acts and awards enclosing four-and-a-half million acres of English open fields and common pastures, two million acres of wild lands and forest and in Wales, during the nineteenth century, an estimated one million acres of upland. Smallholders and tenants near these enclosed lands received little compensation and squatters were summarily evicted with the aid of a virulent propaganda campaign which sought to associate poverty and immorality with common-land farming. W. G. Hoskins and L. Dudley Stamp, in their survey *The Common Lands of England and Wales* (1963), quote a Shropshire reporter to the Board of Agriculture in 1794, who stated what was undoubtedly the typical government attitude when he invited his contemporaries to:

> go round the commons now open, and view the miserable
> huts and poor, ill-cultivated, impoverished spots ...
> which by loss of time both to the man and his family affords
> them a very trifle of independence; this idea leads the man
> to lose many days' work by which he gets a habit of
> indolence; a daughter kept at home to milk a half-starved
> cow, who being open to temptations, soon turns harlot, and
> becomes a distressed ignorant mother instead of making a
> good, useful servant.[2]

Lords of the manor claimed a right to enclose their common lands under an Act of 1235 known as the Statute of Merton. Originally it was intended to improve grazing without in any way diminishing the benefits of common. In the eighteenth and nineteenth centuries, however, enclosure invariably meant private ownership, as lords and wealthy freeholders contrived to make themselves the main beneficiaries of any 'settlement'.

This did not take place everywhere without resistance. Otmoor, an expanse of wetland to the north-east of Oxford, was the common of seven parishes. In 1814 an application to enclose it provoked an uprising of villagers armed with farm implements. They prevented the affixing of statutory notices to the doors of their parish churches. A year later a bill of enclosure was nevertheless passed, prompting speculators to move in, buying out cottagers and financing an expensive scheme for land drainage. Opposition was fierce, but 15 years were to elapse before the prolonged erosion of common rights turned local hostility into mass protest, by which time the threat of violence had become a cause for widespread concern. Embankments were cut and on one occasion 1,000 people marched round the seven-mile perimeter of the moor, breaking down fences as they went. Troops were called out to disperse the 'riot' and 44 demonstrators were arrested. It was the week of St Giles Fair. When the yeomanry entered Oxford they were attacked and the prisoners released. For several years after this débâcle, the dispossessed commoners continued wrecking the bounds. Today Otmoor is protected by the Nature Conservancy Council as a Site of Special Scientific Interest.

Until the late nineteenth century there was little sympathy in Parliament for the plight of commoners and voteless farm labourers. An Inclosure Act of 1845, containing a few token and largely ineffective concessions to the poor, simplified and considerably reduced the cost of the legal processes of enclosure throughout England and Wales. Its only benefit to the average commoner was the stipulation that in any proposal to enclose land, the health, comfort and convenience of local people *should* be taken into consideration and that the commissioners *might* specify the setting aside of an area for the benefit of local inhabitants who wished to take exercise and recreation. The effect of the Act was to make practically all common land worth enclosure. Indeed the government's own Office of Works set an unparalleled example by their dis-afforestation and rental of Crown lands once subject to the rights of common. Speculators gleefully bought up old titles and Crown rights wherever they saw that land values would soar once they had achieved the status of sole owner and user. Commons botanically described in Domesday as *Bruaria*, forests once governed by courts and guarded by reeves and verderers, were to the new owners unprofitable lands unless flattened, drained, cleared of wild animals, gypsies and children and put to 'efficient' agricultural use.

Since before the agricultural revolution of the eighteenth century, uncultivated commons had been described as the 'wastes' of manors. 'Wastes indeed!' declared the radical essayist William Cobbett. 'Give a dog an ill-name. Was Horton Heath a waste? Was it a "waste" when a hundred perhaps of healthy boys and girls were playing there of a Sunday instead of creeping about covered with filth in the alleys of a town?'[3] Cobbett's humanism did not prevail against economic arguments; poor children were small adults, useful for minding machines or crawling up chimneys; play belonged to the idyllic past: the future lay with towns and factories. There was no place in the urban environment for such a frivolity as a playground. When in 1847 the first northern municipal park, designed by Joseph Paxton, was opened in the township of Birkenhead to the financial benefit of those able to buy the building plots on its periphery, no provision whatsoever was made for children to play. The Recreation Grounds Act of 1859 went a little way towards meeting the deficiency, but only in the 1870s, with the publication of Octavia Hill's essays on urban improvement, was the right of working-class children to open-air recreation generally conceded.

By that time the middle classes, the majority of whom already owned gardens or had access to a square, had become aware of the potential of urban remnants of common land as alternative places for relaxation. Romanticism in art and literature showed that a wilderness was beautiful and, if carefully managed – or rather, carefully neglected – could be as desirable as a tended garden or a park laid out to order. City clerks and accountants sought suburban property fronted by land which required neither costly purchase nor radical alteration. They moved to the defence of common rights and titles and the enactment of regulation schemes under the free and friendly guidance of Bob Hunter, Solicitor to the Commons Preservation Society. Their appreciation of open spaces strengthened their sense of community. The first rambling clubs comprised a number of middle-class men who met on Sunday afternoons for vigorous walks on the commons. On weekdays they and their children, as members of a naturalists' club, might use the same commons as their scientific laboratories. The *Song* praising nature's chaos in the early poetry of John Clare, a dispossessed common-land farmer who ended his life penniless, vagrant and lunatic, would have served equally as an anthem for the commons' new devotees, the successful bourgeoisie:

> Swamps of wild rush beds and sloughs squashy traces
> Grounds of rough fallows wi thistle and weed
> Flats and low vallies of king cups and daiseys
> Sweetest of subjects are ye for my reed
> Ye commons left free in the rude rags of nature
> Ye brown heaths be cloathed in furze as ye be
> My wild eye in rapture adores e'ery feature
> Yere as dear as this heart in my bosom to me.[4]

The way of life of the commons' would-be protectors, however, was a threat to the lands they enjoyed. Suburban dwellers demand cheap and efficient transport to their place of work on weekdays and away from the densely populated towns and cities on holidays and at weekends. Today that need is served by motorways; in the nineteenth century it was met by the railway companies. Both have frequently been empowered to slice common land into shreds, and the question arises as to how far public access, even to the heaths, forests, moors and mountains themselves, can be improved without destroying the essential character and beauty of these wild places. Ever since its foundation the Commons Preservation Society had been mainly occupied in mitigating the effects of railways on common land in and about the metropolis, whilst in the Lake District in the 1880s the Reverend Hardie Rawnsley began to oppose the extension of railway lines into the quiet dales. The campaign to protect open spaces spread beyond the major commercial and industrial regions into the remoter parts of the countryside, and was linked to a concern for historic houses, castles and ancient ruins. In 1877 the Society for the Protection of Ancient Buildings was formed, and in 1894 the National Trust.

No adequate account of the Trust's origins can be given without substantial reference to the Commons Preservation Society, which is where our story begins.

Demands to save open spaces for the enjoyment of the general public were made in response to a continuing social crisis caused by the population explosion during the industrial revolution. In the first half of the nineteenth century the population of England and Wales more than doubled, and there was a massive migration from the countryside into the towns and cities. The population became most concentrated wherever trade and manufacturing was expanding, creating new wealth. In consequence, poverty, destitution and overcrowding were prevalent, and the need for open spaces for recreation and fresh air soon became apparent.

That evocative phrase 'the open space movement' embraces several organisations, whose aims have been to secure commons, playgrounds, parks and countryside for the enjoyment of the general public. The first and most effective of these was the Commons Preservation Society, which came into being almost entirely thanks to one man: a young radical who entered Parliament as Member for Reading in 1863, and more than 30 years later published *English Commons and Forests* (1894), a history of the movement he had inspired. Following his education at Eton and Trinity College, Cambridge, George John Shaw-Lefevre became a barrister at the Inner Temple. He was not by nature an outgoing person. Had he been so, perhaps Shaw-Lefevre, later Lord Eversley, would be better known for his achievements in successive Liberal governments, as Secretary to the Board of Trade, then to the Admiralty, and later as First Commissioner of Works. This last appointment enabled him to give the public access to several of London's once privately enjoyed open spaces, including the grounds of Hampton Court, Kew Gardens and parts of Regent's Park. His most abiding monument, however, is the incalculable acreage of common land which, thanks to his consistent advocacy, remains open to the public to this day. The supply by municipal authorities of fresh water, roads and sewers was in due course seen to be a necessity, but the purchase of open spaces for leisure was relegated to a poor second place. Shaw-Lefevre's re-affirmation of common rights in law, however, reduced the value of commons to the private buyer. Their purchase for purposes of public recreation then became an attractive proposition.

The possibility of protecting common land for its recreational value was first fully discussed in Westminster during the Whig administrations of the 1860s. In 1862 considerable concern was expressed by some London MPs at the rapid destruction of the Essex Forest. Three years later, in February 1865, they passed a motion appointing a Select Committee 'to inquire into the best means of preserving for public use the Forests, Commons and Open Spaces in and around the metropolis'. Shaw-Lefevre made what was undoubtedly the most effective speech in the debate, citing various cases in law which had done nothing but confuse the issue as to what leisure rights, if any, the public might have over common grounds.[5] Because of his passionate interest, he was nominated to serve on the Committee.

The issue which had provoked some urgency in the debate in Parliament was not only the continuing loss of the Essex or 'Epping' Forest, but also a more immediate threat to Wimbledon Common. In the autumn of 1864, Lord Spencer, who held title to the manor, felt unable to deal adequately with public demands to drain the Common and clear it of gypsies, vagrants and rubbish heaps. He declared his intention to build on 300 acres, including Putney Heath, and to convert the remaining 700 acres into a public park. It seemed a reasonable proposal. Indeed the Select Committee could not but confirm that Wimbledon and many other London commons were in a deplorable state, almost justifying the actions of lords of the manor who purloined them for building, gravel-mining or for sale to the railway companies. Diminished commons frequently became rubbish dumps and the haunt of undesirable characters; their enclosure could be claimed as a responsible act: prevent uncontrolled access, it was argued, and the nuisance would be abated.

Another approach to the problem, suggested by the Metropolitan Board of Works, was for that authority to buy up the titles to the commons, sell some of the land for building and use the proceeds to maintain open spaces. The Board was eventually to secure Hampstead Heath, by purchasing it from Sir Spencer Maryon Wilson at a cost to ratepayers of £45,000. Shaw-Lefevre, however, moved against such a policy, arguing that if applied all over London it would either incur massive public expenditure, or considerable loss of open space.[6] A sensible way out of the dilemma might be to strengthen common rights at law in a manner which would guarantee both public interest and public access. He and several colleagues put their case in a report which the Select Committee accepted and presented to the House within a month of its formation. The Committee declared the supreme necessity of preserving all remaining London commons for the health and recreation of the people, and, as a sign of patriotism, for the exercises of military volunteer corps.

Looked upon favourably by a Liberal government, Shaw-Lefevre's proposal was cast in the form of a Bill which gave to commoners and ratepayers in London the power to elect, with the approval of the Inclosure Commissioners, Boards of Conservators to manage a common, if need be without the approval of the Lord of the Manor. This measure, known as the Metropolitan Commons Act, was to come into force on 10 August 1866 and although it applied only to an area within a 15-mile radius of Charing Cross, it embraced 180 open spaces comprising well over 10,000 acres. Within its limitations it was a comprehensive piece of legislation. Owners of common land everywhere were alarmed by it, despite the failure of an amendment to extend its influence to suburban areas in other parts of the country.

Lords of the manor feared further protective legislation. Consequently, long-cherished plans for enclosures were hastily re-examined. In Epping Forest new fencing soon lay on the ground for miles, awaiting imminent erection. At Berkhamsted, Plumstead and Tooting fences were put up. Even before the Act of 1866 came into force, however, an organisation outside Parliament was preparing to challenge the powers of enclosing landlords.[7]

A preliminary meeting of an extra-parliamentary group took place on 19 July 1865, in the final stages of a general election. It seemed likely that the Whigs would again form a government. The meeting was convened at Shaw-Lefevre's chambers in the Inner Temple to discover how best to assist commoners in the defence of their rights at law. Those who attended were the liberal/radical elite. Apart from Shaw-Lefevre, two other barristers of the Temple were present: the Christian Socialist Thomas Hughes MP, now best remembered as the author of the Victorian classic *Tom Brown's Schooldays*, and Charles Edward Pollock. Both these men enjoyed highly successful legal careers. Hughes and Shaw-Lefevre were accompanied by several of their colleagues from the House of Commons, including Sir Thomas Fowell Buxton and his brother Charles (sons of a father who had been a fierce opponent of the slave trade and a renowned advocate of penal reform), an eminent lawyer, Mr Burrell, and William Francis Cowper, later Lord Mount Temple. The star of the gathering was the new Member of Parliament for Westminster, John Stuart Mill. His presence was a coup for the organisers as, like most of the economists of his time, Mill had once been strongly in favour of enclosures. It was on a visit to the historians George and Harriet Grote, who lived near Burnham Beeches, that the importance of maintaining commons for the cottage economy of the poor suddenly dawned upon him. He saw for himself the plight of the villagers of East Burnham who were suffering the involuntary extinguishment of their common rights under threat of eviction from Lady Grenville, the lord of the manor. That experience so affected Mill as to make him want to forget that he had ever advocated the wholesale conversion of common land to private use.

> I have all my life been strongly impressed with the importance of preserving as much as possible of such free space for healthful exercise and for the enjoyment of natural beauty as the growth of population and cultivation has still left to us. The desire to engross the whole surface of the earth in the mere production of the greatest quantity of food and the materials of manufacture, I consider to be founded on a mischievously narrow conception of the requirements of human nature. I therefore highly applaud the formation of the Commons Preservation Society, and am prepared to co-operate in the promotion of its objects in any manner which lies in my power.[8]

This small group arranged further meetings in various parts of the city to win the support of those with most influence. Between them they raised £1,400 to finance the new cause and within six months preparations were under way for the proper constitution of their Society. An advertisement on the front page of *The Times* announced a public meeting chaired by the Lord Mayor of London, to take place at the Mansion House at one o'clock on 24 January 1866. Among those on the list of eminent sponsors were the Bishop of London, the Deans of Westminster and St Paul's, a dozen Members of Parliament, several Aldermen, four Fellows of the Royal Society, Professor Henry Fawcett MP, whose work for the cause in Parliament would prove to be decisive, and other prominent representatives of the political, legal, medical and scientific fraternities. The prospect of losing common land had aroused widespread concern.[9]

At the Mansion House meeting, the Lord Mayor, Benjamin Samuel Phillips, began the proceedings by reminding his audience of the chronic need for public access to open spaces in a city of three million inhabitants with 'its narrow streets, confined courts, smoke and other evils'. There then followed a speech by John Locke, MP for Southwark, who moved a resolution that 'the preservation of the commons and open spaces in the neighbourhood of the metropolis was absolutely essential to the health and recreation of the people'; a sign that the Commons Preservation Society was to set its sights beyond the boundaries defined by the Metropolitan Commons Act. This first resolution was passed unanimously. A second motion proposed by Shaw-Lefevre effectively defined the CPS as a political pressure group, to make legislators realise in future the public need for lawful access to open spaces. 'The law had been very chary of allowing anything like a public right' declared Shaw-Lefevre: whilst recognising the right of a village to its green, there had been no legal recognition of 'an analogy between the village and its green and the great city and its commons'. The immediate danger to common lands and forests was not always wholesale enclosure, but a gradual 'sweating' – a piecemeal reduction by the operation of a 'rolling fence'. It was Tom Hughes who seconded this resolution, which again was passed unanimously. The meeting ended with the Lord Mayor, on behalf of everyone present, signing a petition to both Houses of Parliament, advocating proper legal status for public access to commons.[10]

Few of those who had attended the meeting that day could have guessed what an extraordinary situation would confront the CPS within a few weeks of its formation.

On a ridge 26 miles north of London lies a crescent-shaped wilderness, four miles long and a half a mile wide; 1,200 acres of grasses, gorse, ferns, heather and woods supporting abundant wildlife. For centuries it had provided wild fruits as food, grazing and litter for animals and fuel from its fallen timber; a natural harvest which was the communal property of nearby villagers. Once an integral part of the Chiltern Forest, this land was governed locally by a folk-moot which in Anglo-Saxon times met in the precincts of Berkhamsted Castle.

An attempt to enclose the area on the eve of the Civil War was forestalled when inhabitants of nearby Northchurch 'pull'd downe and carried away the hedges and rayles and fences'.[11] No doubt the villagers felt they had triumphed, but only the uncertain political climate of the time allowed the ringleaders to go unpunished when they were arraigned at the Bar of the House of Lords. During the following three centuries Berkhamsted Common was 'sweated' by the Egerton family, Earls and Dukes of Bridgewater, who claimed the estate to the east known as Ashridge Park, now owned by the National Trust. They permitted several illegal enclosures under the pretext of 'improvement'.

In 1853 however, after bitter litigation, the House of Lords ruled that the Bridgewater entitlement was invalid. The real heir was Lord Brownlow, the ailing 11-year-old son of Lady Marion Alford, a woman whose ambition more than compensated for her son's frailty. He and his mother took up residence at Ashridge and began to plan the total enclosure of that part of the common immediately adjoining the estate. Trenches were cut across bridleways to stop the passage of villagers' carts, and the estate manager, William Paxton, started negotiations with commoners in Berkhamsted to buy out their rights and exchange them for a recreation ground on a swamp by the river Bulbourne, between the town and the railway station. The deal was advertised by Walter Hazell, a local grocer who set great store by his trade with the manor house.

Opponents of this miserable bargain were few, but among them was one commoner wealthy enough to withstand local pressures. Augustus Smith not only possessed land in Berkhamsted but also held a lease of the Scilly Isles, and had personally done much to improve conditions for the inhabitants. He had fought the Duchy of Cornwall and the Crown to protect rights of access to the foreshore of the Cornish coast. Smith did not entirely disapprove of enclosures provided they were carried out legally through the offices of the Parliamentary Inclosure Commissioners. In a letter

from Bournemouth dated 10 November 1865, young Lord Brownlow had given him to understand that enclosure with the Commissioners' approval was being given serious consideration.[12]

Be that as it may, Lady Marion was more grasping. She lived in
fear that, in her own words, 'the society for the protection of waste
lands and commons [the CPS] had threatened to widen the radius
drawn round London for preventing enclosures under Act of
Parliament'. She convened a meeting with William Paxton and her
solicitors, Messrs Grover & Stocken. They resolved to lose no time
in enclosing more than 400 acres of the Common, 'and leave it to
anyone who should oppose us to prove that we had not the right to
do so'.[13] The following February the fences were erected.

News of what had taken place caused something of a stir in
London. The Common was outside the jurisdiction of the
proposed Metropolitan Commons Act, but if the CPS was not to
appear impotent its officers must take action. Shaw-Lefevre
contacted Augustus Smith. They took advice from Philip
Lawrence, the Society's solicitor, and decided at once 'to resort to
the old practice of abating the enclosure by the forcible removal of
all the fences, in a manner which would be a demonstration, and an
assertion of right, not less conspicuous than their erection'.[14]

So it was that on the night of 6 March 1866, 120 navvies were
secretly transported by chartered railway train from Euston
station on what is now the well-travelled northern line through
Watford and Hemel Hempstead. The train did not stop at
Berkhamsted but continued past the castle ruins and eventually
halted at one-thirty in the morning at Tring Station.

Here the operation nearly came to grief. The navvies disem-
barked, but as there was no leader to be seen, they wandered about
aimlessly on the platform. A Mr Duncan, who was supposed to be
in charge, having correctly surmised that this would be a delicate
operation, delegated his responsibilities to an assistant. However,
they both got drunk at Euston and missed the train.

Fortunately, someone higher in the chain of command was at
hand. His name remains a mystery, but in a mock epic poem which
was published in *Punch* a fortnight later it was hinted that Augustus Smith himself was on the train.[15] Shaw-Lefevre may also have
been an eyewitness. At all events it appears that Philip Lawrence's
confidential clerk, George Micklewright, stepped into the breach.
A carriageful of tools was unloaded and 'a procession was formed
at the station – each man shouldering a crowbar or other imple-
ment'. The task-force then set out by moonlight along the road
from the station, past the peaceful village of Aldbury and on to

Berkhamsted Common from the north. The danger of alerting potential opposition was thus avoided.

It was not long before they encountered two long fences consisting of five-foot high posts joined one to another by broad metal bands set at close intervals. In groups of a dozen the navvies set to work. The substantial joints of the railings were loosened with hammers and chisels, and crowbars used to lift out the posts. By six o'clock the posts, neatly wrapped in their metal bands, were stacked at intervals across the ground. The Common was liberated.

Grocer Hazell in his horse and cart was the first on the scene. In response to his heated demand for an explanation of the night's work the labourers good-humouredly offered to cool him down in the nearby Grand Junction Canal. Instead he was eventually induced to tap the barrels of beer he was carrying in the cart. By seven, news of what had happened reached William Paxton. He arrived to see for himself the almost unbelievable loss of a desirable extension to Ashridge Park. He was very upset and stood raving at the onlookers and making dire threats of action against 'trespassers'. As the day wore on, people flocked to the scene.

In carriages, gigs, dogcarts and on foot; gentry, shopkeepers, husbandmen, women and children, at once tested the reality of what they saw by strolling over and squatting on the Common and taking away morsels of gorse to prove, as they said, that the place was their own again.

The *Bucks Advertiser* described the reclamation as 'one of the most decided and vigorous protests against alleged usurpation which have occurred in our prosaic, peaceful and order-loving times'.[16] A few days' planning by the leaders of the CPS had accomplished in one night what generations of downtrodden and dispossessed farm labourers had failed to achieve in more than three centuries; this victory saw the dawn of a new and at last successful offensive in the long battle against illegal fences and Inclosure Act hedges.

Berkhamsted was only the beginning. By the end of the year the CPS was advising litigants on the preservation of commons at Hampstead, Wimbledon and Wandsworth and actions would soon commence over land at Plumstead, Tooting, Coulsdon, Dartford and Banstead. The Society was now run from an office at 29 Parliament Street, strategically close to the Houses of Parliament.

Until this time, the judiciary had been uncritical of the enclosure movement, so the CPS planned its strategy very carefully, arranging the order in which the cases should be tried and choosing Courts of Equity where the presiding judges were known to be sympathetic to the new cause. In this way, judges such as John Romilly and George Jessel, both of whom had been Liberal MPs, were enabled to adjudicate in favour of the Society.

The court case that ensued over Berkhamsted demonstrates the CPS's typical legal tactic of selecting just one or two commoners with a strong will and adequate financial resources to fight an enclosure.

Within three days of the Common being forcibly re-opened, Augustus Smith found himself on a charge of causing damage by trespass, brought by Lord Brownlow. Brownlow's solicitor tried to weight the evidence, arguing that the common right could have been more amicably tested had the defendant simply removed just one rail of the disputed fencing. In the preliminary hearing before the trial Smith was accused of 'lawlessness', but Judge Romilly, who presided, was not slow to see that Brownlow's legal advisers were attempting to evade the issue of common rights by raising prejudice against the defendant. Their attack failed. In the light of what ensued, the decision to dismantle all fences proved wise, for before the trial could begin Lord Brownlow died, and under rules of procedure the case could not be revived by his successor. It was stalemate. Augustus Smith found himself liable for costs, but at least the Common was open. To consolidate the position, the CPS encouraged Smith to bring a lawsuit against the Brownlow trustees based upon the infringement of his common rights. Four years later those rights were legally vindicated. The final judgement and the fact that the land in question had been kept unfenced ensured that Berkhamsted Common was safe for public access.[17]

The conflict between some Lords and commoners in London and the surrounding areas now became ferocious. In the same month as the liberation of Berkhamsted Common, the Provost and scholars of Queen's College, Oxford, no doubt fearing a catastrophic drop in the potential building-site value of their Plumstead Manor lands, erected fences round what they regarded as their exclusive property. In response, the inhabitants of East Wickham arranged a meeting with the CPS, formed an action committee and immediately organised a demolition party. On 4 August 1866, the fences having been pulled down, Julian Goldsmid, prospective parliamentary candidate for Rochester, and three other commoners started a successful action against the College.[18]

Henry Peek, the Tory MP for mid-Surrey, another powerful recruit to the CPS, headed a committee of his constituents living near Wimbledon Common. They began court proceedings on 1 December. Peek filed a Bill in Chancery restraining Lord Spencer from allowing the Common to be used as the site for a brick works. Meanwhile, in nearby Hampstead, another committee was formed to defend the famous Heath. In this case also, proceedings were begun in Chancery.

The confident manner in which the CPS had set about the reclamation of Berkhamsted Common won it support from many quarters. In 1867 a two-penny pamphlet entitled 'A Glance at the Commons and Open Spaces near London' gives a list of branch committees, most of which had been formed for the defence of particular sites.[19] So sudden was the great wave of enthusiasm for old commons that the CPS office was now inundated with enquiries. An enormous amount of legal and historical information had to be accumulated and filed.

The laws governing various usages of common land had hitherto often simply been assumed, and remained unrecorded. Where they had been accurately set down in writing, the language employed was generally a form of Old English or Latin, using terminology which no longer had much currency. The words themselves were descriptive of a lost world of communal land usage: *pannage*, the common right to graze pigs on beech and acorn mast and other natural foods; *turbary*, the right to dig peat; *piscary*, the right to fish; *herbage* and *agistment*, the rights of pasture; *stinting*, the control of the right of grazing by limiting the number of beasts permitted to be turned out on one common; *estovers*, the right to take naturally-fallen underwood from a common, and sometimes also the branches cut from pollarded trees – these might be used as *heybote* for the repair of fences or *firebote* for fuel. *Housebote* was a right to take large pieces of timber for the building and maintenance of cottages and the renovation of agricultural implements. In all this, as Shaw-Lefevre had repeatedly pointed out, there was no clearly documented right of *leisure* over common land, although as in the case of village greens, custom might have sanctioned it. For centuries many commons had been used regularly for fairs, markets, prize-fights, games and dancing. In a court of law, however, it was necessary to prove that the specific custom referred to had been officially granted. The survival of commons as public open spaces in the nineteenth century was in almost every instance dependent upon the retrieval of old documents, particularly the Court Rolls of various manors, in order to gain evidence either of such a grant or of the existence of a common right that had not been bought out by compensation. This research could be expensive, and a more thorough understanding of common rights was urgently needed to support each individual case.

Once he had joined the CPS, Henry Peek immediately saw the need to initiate an in-depth study of common rights which would assist the Society in its moral and historical claims. He understood that legal success depended on general as well as particular argument. At the same time he wanted to attract the most able legal minds to the cause of common-land conservation. He therefore placed a newspaper advertisement offering prizes totalling £400 for the best essays on the subject of 'Commons and the means of Preserving them for the Public'.[20] This notice caught the eye of Bob Hunter, an articled clerk, who was to become the open space movement's greatest legal advocate.

CHAPTER 2

Robert Hunter

Addington Square is one of those little backwaters of South London miraculously spared redevelopment. Several old plane trees shade the large central lawn, which in Spring is a blaze of crocuses. The varied architectural style of the surrounding houses lends to the square a distinctive charm, and enhances an open space planned originally for the sole enjoyment of the residents. In spite of the proximity of the busy Camberwell Road, it remains a peaceful oasis. Here, in an elegant three-storey house, Robert Hunter was born on 27 October 1844, the first child of Robert Lachlan and Anne Hunter.[1]

Robert Lachlan Hunter, who as a child had run away to sea to join the whaling fleet, had by the time of his son's birth become a master mariner. His sea-going career had been profitable enough to allow him to establish his own mercantile business in London, and he now lived at home. The family's prosperous, insulated and well-ordered life was, however, soon to be disrupted.

London was frequently swept by cholera epidemics, which killed many of those living in its poor and overcrowded districts, and just before his third birthday Bob Hunter became seriously ill. He slowly recovered, but remained subdued and prone to severe forms of every childish illness.

Social unrest at this period posed a threat to security. Chartist gangs roamed the streets and the residents of Addington Square hid their jewellery in the water butts. Robert Hunter enrolled as a special constable to assist Peel's Metropolitan Police force in dealing with the riots. On one occasion in 1848 young Bob and his pregnant mother only just reached the relative safety of their home before a violent mob invaded the Camberwell Road. Fortunately the violence of the Chartist movement was short-lived.

In 1853, in more settled times, the Hunter family moved to 10 De Crespigny Terrace, Denmark Hill, a tall, north-facing house over-looking fields. From the top rooms, on a clear day, there was a superb view across London as far as Highgate. The back garden, with its vine, sunflowers, roses and an old hawthorn tree, was a magnificent playground for children. Bob was now at preparatory school, but at weekends he and his sister Ann were taken to concerts, museums and book clubs, and on one memorable day, to the Crystal Palace to see Blondin, the famous acrobat, wheeling a barrow along the high wire. For holidays they went for three weeks each year to the seaside at Hastings, Harwich or Brighton. On several occasions they stayed at Dorking, where the children spent hours in the wilderness of Ranmore Common. In 1860 they visited the Scottish highlands, and about this time Bob discovered his enthusiasm for botany. As time went on this interest was translated into an understanding of the urgent need to protect unculti-vated land, with its indigenous plant and wild life.

The Hunters hoped that their son would enter one of the profes-sions, and planned his education accordingly. After prep school he was sent as a day boy to the Charles Peter Mason School for Boys, and during his last year there his parents engaged Leonard Seeley, a barrister and Cambridge graduate, to give him extra coaching for the final examinations. At the age of 17 he was awarded a place at University College, London.

Although a confirmed member of the Church of England, at one time even considering ordination, while he was at university Bob Hunter also occasionally attended the evening service at Claylands Congregational Chapel. Here he heard the ideas of Christian Socialism expounded by the Reverend Baldwin Brown, which focused his mind on the issues underlying Chartist unrest. The Chartists had petitioned for universal male suffrage, for payment of MPs, and for the abolition of property qualifications to enable any man, regardless of wealth, to stand for Parliament. Some of them had established agricultural communes in various parts of the country, but these were not a success. Their longing to return to the land remained unsatisfied.

In 1864 Bob Hunter gained his BA Honours degree, with Firsts in Logic and Moral Philosophy, and was encouraged by his father to enrol as an articled clerk with a firm of solicitors in Holborn. The days and months with Eyre Lawson & Long turned out to be purgatory. He found the work totally uninteresting, and did not share the other clerks' fondness for betting to relieve the boredom.

Reading for a Master's degree in his own time, each evening he would return home, retreat into his study and work in sullen isolation. His increasing solitariness worried his family. Convinced that he was in need of a complete break, his mother and sister insisted on taking him for an extra week's holiday. They stayed at the King's Arms Hotel near Hampton Court where at dusk, when the hundreds of day visitors to Bushy Park had left, the deer would come down to feed from their hands. His sister remembered this moment of tranquillity vividly, and recorded it at some length in an account of their childhood written in later life.

Soon after this brief respite, the family moved to Carrick House, Surbiton, but in spite of the long hours which now had to be spent travelling each day to his work, Bob did not have the courage to leave home. Desperate to occupy his mind, his eye was caught by a newspaper advertisement for a competition organised by the Commons Preservation Society. Cash prizes were offered for the best essays on 'means of preserving common lands for the enjoyment of the public'. He determined to try his hand, and spent the winter evenings in research and writing. In the spring of 1867 he submitted his entry, and about the same time celebrated his engagement to Emily Browning, a childhood sweetheart, whom he married two years later.

These events prompted a noticeable change in his personality. Shedding his previous introversion, Bob Hunter became the genial character who was never to lose heart in the campaigns and causes of the open space movement.

It was evident to the officers of the CPS that Bob Hunter's 15,000-word essay demonstrated a comprehensive understanding of rights of common. His reasoning was sound and he argued convincingly in favour of extending the provisions in the Metropolitan Commons Act to open spaces within the vicinity of all major towns and cities. More to the point, the adjudicators noted that he approved of the CPS policy of direct action against lords of the manor, described by the essayist as 'active in aggression'.

The mode of procedure will of course differ in different cases, but one suggestion may be made. Any commoner whose rights are molested is clearly entitled to throw down the whole fencing or other obstruction erected. It may also be mentioned that, in many cases, the Crown has rights of forest over waste lands, as, for example, over Epping

Forest, and if these rights were properly insisted on, approvements, [i.e. enclosures] must in such places cease. Every possible step should at once be taken; and the owners of the soil, if they persist in acts of violence, should be forced before a Court of Law or Equity.[2]

The essay as a whole so impressed the judges that, although it was not awarded first prize, it was nevertheless chosen as one of six to be prepared for publication. The first prize was awarded to John Maidlow, a barrister of Lincoln's Inn and Fellow of Queen's College, Oxford, the very college which was attempting enclosure, under the Statute of Merton, of the common lands in the manor of Plumstead. 'It would have been well for the interests of the College', wrote Shaw-Lefevre, 'if its Fellows had followed his advice in preference to that of their lawyers.'[3]

Maidlow proved that the enactment of the Court of Henry III held at Merton was not the last word in favour of enclosure that many titleholders assumed it to be. Careful examination of the proclamation showed that it was severely limiting of 'approvements' and applied exclusively to common of pasture; it could not be construed to interfere with other rights, such as *piscary, estovers* and *turbary*. It allowed for enclosure only in so far as such action left sufficient pasture for commoners' needs, without any lessening of their convenience. Both Maidlow and Bob Hunter argued that the Statute of Merton should nevertheless be repealed.

Within a few months of the publication of the essays, Philip Lawrence, Honorary Solicitor to the CPS and its adviser in the Berkhamsted case, was approached by the Liberal government and offered the post of Solicitor to the Office of Works. This appointment, amongst other things, would give him overall advisory responsibility for the department managing Crown forests, woods and commons. Acceptance of the offer would render impartiality impossible and another solicitor for the CPS would have to be found, preferably one with a particular interest in open space legal work. The committee turned to its list of winning essayists. Bob Hunter, not quite 24, would soon be qualified. He was offered the post and accepted it. Released at last from the tedium of his articles, he moved to Lincoln's Inn Fields.

Until the formation of the CPS, rights of common had never been defended systematically. The outcome of every case was uncertain and Bob Hunter took up his new appointment in the middle of a crisis which had been partly caused by the very policy which the CPS had adopted.

The problem was highlighted on a 60-acre common in Tooting Graveney, where a Mr W. S. Thompson, who had bought title to the manor, had illegally enclosed 25 acres. Local residents, emboldened by the news from Berkhamsted and Plumstead, had begun breaking through the fences where and when it suited them. Direct action of this sort could be construed as an offence against public order, as it had been at Otmoor, and this time the CPS would be held to blame. To regularise the situation, three of the commoners were advised to bring a private prosecution against the encloser. Three years elapsed before the case was finally resolved. When it came to trial Judge Romilly, after an eleven-day hearing, ruled in favour of the commoners. The defendant appealed, and only after a further six days' hearing before Judge Hatherley did the plaintiffs finally win. Victory, however, was soured by Hatherley's ruling that they should bear their own considerable legal costs. Perhaps the way the commoners had gone about the vindication of their rights had earned them some judicial disapproval.

Negotiations in the dispute over Wimbledon Common, Wandsworth Common and Putney Heath were undertaken by the CPS in calmer circumstances. Earl Spencer, lord of the manor, while sympathetic to the question of public access, was eager to enclose a large part of these common lands. Bob Hunter felt strongly that the whole area should remain open for public recreation. The manorial rolls for Wimbledon from the time of Edward IV onwards were still in existence and appeared to give considerable powers to the lord of the manor. Local land conveyancing documents told a different story however, making frequent and specific reference to common rights. It was on these documents that Bob Hunter based his case. He argued so convincingly that Lord Spencer felt obliged to give way, and invited him to draw up Regulation Bills for all the commons, to be presented to Parliament. The commons would be governed by committees of local residents known as Conservators, and the maintenance of them would be financed by the levy of a special rate. The Metropolitan Board, local government authority for all London, subsequently employed Bob Hunter to negotiate the purchase of manorial title to the lands from Earl Spencer for £25 an acre. Although not strictly within the terms of CPS policy, this deal made the future of these open spaces more secure.[4]

The position of CPS Solicitor was eminently suited to Bob Hunter's temperament; the work required both legal acumen and a commitment to the cause. A staunch Liberal and a member of the Reform Club, he could express his idealism in the open space movement without being directly involved in the heat of politics. He established a good relationship with the CPS executive committee and soon felt at ease with its senior members. They did not hesitate to ask his opinions and seek his advice.

At a meeting of the CPS executive soon after his appointment, Bob Hunter met Henry Fawcett for the first time. He was to become a lifelong friend. In 1863, two years before he entered politics as a Liberal MP, Fawcett had been elected Professor of Political Economy at Cambridge. His first published lectures dealt with the losses suffered by agricultural labourers' families as a result of the extinguishment of their common rights. Any compensation that might be awarded, he argued, could be dissipated by the first recipients, to the permanent deprivation of their descendants. They would then become dependent upon the more efficient but degradingly exploitative agricultural system which took the place of subsistence farming. In addition to taking a means of living from farm workers during times of unemployment, the enclosure of commons robbed villagers as well as townsfolk of their leisure grounds. Roads, observed Fawcett, were fast becoming the only playgrounds for many children.[5]

Fawcett's passionate desire that the countryside should be accessible to all classes is made the more poignant by the fact that he had been blinded in a shooting accident at the age of 25. Only in his imagination could he see the forests and open spaces he wished to save. He remained a sportsman: riding, fishing, walking and rowing and in winter skating 50 or 60 miles a day on the frozen fens.

> On the wide open spaces he would skate quite alone, guided
> only by the sound of his companions' voices and skates.
> When his daughter was about nine, she guided him in this
> fashion, whistling to give him notice of her whereabouts.[6]

The partnership of Fawcett and Bob Hunter was to prove a powerful force in the CPS campaign, bringing to an abrupt end the systematic enclosure of some 25,000 acres of common land each year.

An unprecedented opportunity to postpone all 'legal' enclosures presented itself at the beginning of a new parliamentary session in 1868. The Inclosure Commissioners introduced their annual Bill, fully expecting that it would go through on the nod, as usual. They considered that their duty was simply to gain parliamentary approval of the private agreements reached between lords of the manor and commoners; commons were not public property and the issue of access for recreation did not therefore concern them. The Bill scheduled a modest 7,000 acres for enclosure, of which a grand total of three acres was to be reserved for recreation and six for allotments. It contained an 'approvement' plan for the Common of Wisley, on the road from Kingston to Guildford.

Under pressure from local residents, some London MPs objected strongly to the inclusion of Wisley and on this pretext Fawcett used every means at his disposal to block the Commissioners' entire Bill. When the time came for its Third Reading, he and a small group of supporters, including Tom Hughes, John Locke and Sir Charles Dilke, gave notice that they would move for its recommittal, in a bid to obtain a larger acreage for allotments. The government, intent on getting the measure through as quickly as possible, set it down at the end of the Order Paper for every available day. The CPS supporters were thus obliged to remain in the Chamber every night until two or three o'clock in the morning. On one occasion, when Fawcett sent word that he was ill, requesting a further postponement of the motion, the Government Chief Whip seized his opportunity and placed the Bill on the Order Paper none the less, in clear breach of parliamentary custom. Fortunately, Fawcett had been advised not to take automatic postponement for granted and in spite of his sickness, took his place on the Liberal benches. 'The Whip started "like a guilty thing surprised" on the apparition of Fawcett in the lobby.'[7] A formal assurance of fair play in future then permitted him to return to his bed.

The Annual Inclosure Bill was eventually brought on at a reasonable hour. Fawcett succeeded in getting a resolution passed which authorised the appointment of a Select Committee to consider the workings of the Inclosure Commission and the expediency of better provision for recreation and allotments. He used his influence to secure a majority of CPS sympathisers on the committee, William Harcourt, Henry Peek and Fawcett himself among them, with William Cowper, a founder member of the Society, as Chairman. Fawcett then cross-examined witnesses, establishing the injustice of the tiny acreage reserved for recreation. During the next seven years every effort of the Commissioners to secure the passage of further Bills was successfully resisted. Meanwhile, Bob Hunter, through the courts, was furthering a plan to save Epping Forest, London's largest common. This was to prove a milestone in conservation history. The court case which ensued was conducted as if it were a major public enquiry.

At the time of the Norman invasion the English countryside consisted mainly of woodlands, plains, heaths and marshes, with sparse clearings for cattle and other livestock. After the Conquest all land was in the gift of the king, to be parcelled out to his tenants-in-chief. There was no absolute freehold, and lords of the manor were obliged to provide services to the Crown in return for their grants of land. Irrespective of these grants, the Crown designated as Royal Forests whole areas of countryside rich in deer and game. The land around Epping was part of the Royal Forest of Essex, sometimes called Waltham Forest after the great monastery at its centre. It is now London's most valuable recreation ground: 6,000 acres of woodland and natural pasture, a twelve-mile shaft of open space penetrating the metropolis and stretching from Epping in the north to Wanstead in the south. At its edges are breaks and isolated clearings known as driftways, left between the enclosures so that grazing stock could be driven into the central pastures.[8]

Two interests were served in the creation of a Royal Forest. The monarch claimed the entire area as his hunting ground for game whereas the commoners depended on it for their livelihood, harvesting the woods and 'enlarging' under the right of *agistment*, that is, turning out marked animals to graze and forage, thus fattening them and at the same time loosening the soil to encourage re-seeding. In *A Treatise of the Laws of the Forest* published in 1665, John Manwood states the Crown's view of such lands as

> a certain Territory of wooddy grounds and fruitful paftures, priviledged for wild beafts and fowls of Forest, Chafe and Warren, to reft and abide in, in the fafe protection of the King, for his princely delight and pleafure.[9]

This deceptively idyllic picture concealed a harsh system of justice. Mutilation or death were the penalties for commoners convicted of poaching in the king's wildwood until in 1217 *Charta Forestâ* (an extension of *Magna Charta*) extracted from King John a more humane code. Even so, forest laws were still a byword for severity. The erection of buildings and the taking of timber were rigorously controlled. Cottagers were not allowed to build fences high enough to keep the deer out of their gardens. In the 'fence month', 15 days before and after midsummer day, commoners were obliged to remove their stock from the forest, so as not to interfere with the deer breeding. The Royal Lord Warden and the Verderers, assisted by master keepers, foresters, agisters and regarders, enforced these regulations.

The pressure of increased population, more efficient agriculture and the decline of Royal hunts, changed all this. Legally or otherwise, Royal Forests were diminished and their ancient system of management fell into disuse. From an area estimated in the reign of Charles I as 60,000 acres, Essex Forest was reduced, according to a Report of the Land Revenue Commission of 1793, to a mere 9,000 acres, mostly south of Epping. The Commissioners noted that the forest was frequented by Londoners from the East End for recreation, and on that account ought not to be entirely destroyed, but even so they recommended a continuing sale of Crown rights, thereby facilitating enclosure.

In 1851 the government itself, through the Office of Woods and Forests, cleared 2,000 acres around Hainault, said to have contained the most beautiful trees in Essex. The land was divided up and rented as farms, leaving 55 acres for 'health and exercise'. Anyone claiming to have title in the remaining 7,000 acres was offered Crown rights at less than £5 an acre, including those who had enclosed the land illegally. During a debate in the House of Commons in 1864 William Gladstone, as Chancellor of the Exchequer, zealously reducing the national debt by all possible means, gave wholehearted approval to the entire disposal of Epping Forest. 'As for fresh air', he declared, 'the people of London are not the only persons for whom that is good ... if the claim being made [for open spaces] is admitted, the inhabitants of other parts of England, living in crowded houses and narrow streets, are equally entitled.'[10] An admirer of the sparsity of Greek classical landscape, Gladstone had no great love of thick woodland. In the bracing air of his estate at Hawarden he spent many happy hours felling trees with one of the axes in his collection.

The largest illegal enclosure of what was left of Epping Forest took place in the Manor of Loughton. The lord, the Reverend John Whittaker Maitland, was also rector of the parish – a 'squarson'. Having bought Crown rights, Maitland, without recourse to the Inclosure Commissioners, fenced off 1,300 acres. His parishioners were left with nine acres for 'the good of their health'.

Such pastoral care was not appreciated by families who traced their ancestry in Loughton through many generations. They continued to claim the right to lop the trees for winter fuel. In November 1865, 72-year-old Tom Willingale made a way through the fence carrying an axe and subsisted, as he had always done, by selling the firewood he gathered to his neighbours. He was summoned before the court of petty sessions for injuring the trees, but his case was dismissed; he pleaded a commoner's right. Willingale and some of his neighbours continued to cut branches throughout the winter, until early the following year his son and two nephews were brought before the Bench at Waltham for the same offence, and fined. They refused to pay, and were sentenced to a week's hard labour in Ilford Jail. The CPS decided to make the Loughton enclosures a test case and advised Tom Willingale to file a Bill of Complaint in Chancery against Maitland.[11]

As soon as the CPS took up this case, 'The Forest' became a major issue. Public meetings were organised in the East End, and Gladstone, on becoming Prime Minister in 1868, transferred the Crown rights that remained unsold from the Office of Woods to the Office of Works, giving the impression that henceforth the woods, swales and glades of Epping would be treated with the same respect afforded to a municipal park. This was window-dressing. The recent enclosures, in Bob Hunter's eyes, remained no less an offence in law. In the Spring of the following year the CPS presented to the government a 'May Day Memorial' urging legal proceedings against 211 enclosers and the institution of a new scheme of forest management.[12] Responding to this document, the Chancellor of the Exchequer, Robert Lowe, declared that he had no intention of setting money aside for such a change of policy. He described Gladstone's conciliatory attitude over the issue as very 'oracular ... intended to please everyone'.

The matter simmered for nine months, after which time Fawcett, much to the embarrassment of his party's front bench, moved an Address in the House of Commons appealing directly to the Queen, praying Her Majesty to defend the rights of her Crown and save the Forest. He attacked the sale of Crown rights for a sum which 'is scarcely visible to the naked eye. Ten times as much might have been saved ... by abolishing a sinecure officer such as the Lord Privy Seal, and certainly, one may add, with less regret to lovers of the beautiful.'[13] Gladstone was now even more conciliatory, or so it seemed, and promised a Bill which would protect the Forest.

The Bill, when it arrived, was not quite what the CPS was seeking. In addition to the 4,000 acres of Crown rights already sold, a further 2,000 acres would be offered to titleholders and 400 acres to commoners. Some 600 acres, less than a tenth of the unploughed Forest, would be reserved for public recreation. When asked to comment, Bob Hunter declared flatly that the measure was 'in fact an enclosure Bill, not one for the preservation of the Forest ... It would be far better that Epping Forest should remain as it is than that such a Bill should pass.'[14]

On 23 July 1870, seven members of the CPS Executive met to

discuss the matter. Towards the close of their deliberations Mill moved that 'the Society, considering the Bill introduced by the Government as in direct opposition to the principles for the assertion of which the Society was constituted, do resist it to the utmost.' Andrew Johnston, MP for Essex, moved an amendment 'that the principle of the Bill may be held to be the assertion that some settlement is desirable, and therefore it is not desirable to oppose the Second Reading'.[15] This amendment was lost by a single vote; Mill's resolution was carried. Fawcett straightway set off for the House of Commons to give notice that he would move rejection on the Second Reading. The government, fearing a defeat, promptly withdrew the Bill on a technicality.

A short time later, to Bob Hunter's horror, Tom Willingale died before his case could be heard in court. Fresh enclosures were made on the southernmost clearing of the Forest known as Wanstead Flats and there was a storm of protest. In the House of Commons W. F. Cowper, then President of the CPS, introduced yet another Address along the lines of that first presented by Fawcett. The government suffered a crushing defeat by 197 votes to 96, and as a result were forced to set up a Royal Commission.

More important than the debates in Parliament was the selection of a commoner sufficiently determined to fight the enclosures to the bitter end. In the course of his researches, Bob Hunter discovered that the Corporation of London owned an estate of 200 acres at Little Ilford in the manor of Wanstead, bought for use as a cemetery. The local authority itself therefore possessed rights of common within the Forest. At the time, the Corporation was threatened with demands for a single municipal government and was therefore not averse to a proposal which could demonstrate the effectiveness of its existing constitution. The CPS persuaded the city fathers to allow Bob Hunter to conduct a case for the Forest under supervision of the City Solicitor. On 20 June 1871 notices were posted on trees within the enclosures of Wanstead Flats. These warned the lord of the manor and all whom it might concern that legal action was about to be taken unless all fences were immediately removed.

Bob Hunter was not negotiating to save just part of the Forest. With the legal department of the Corporation of London at his disposal, his sights were now firmly set beyond the manors of Loughton and Wanstead. His examination of the records of the Forest Courts convinced him that the same rights of pasture existed throughout the whole area. It had been maintained by the lords of the manors that rights in the Forest were manorial only, that is to say, enjoyed by the tenants of each manor separately.

History suggested otherwise. Common rights in a forest were *not* the same as those elsewhere. They were granted by the Crown as compensation for the burden of forest laws. A Royal Forest was in fact one great common with its own ordinance overriding the manorial system. It followed therefore that one commoner could contest and upset the enclosures made by the lords of manor in every part of the same forest. This conception of forestal common rights dictated Bob Hunter's next move: on 21 August proceedings were begun against 16 of the lords of manors. A Bill was filed in Chancery on behalf of 'The Commissioners of Sewers of the City of London', the department in which the Ilford estate was vested.[16]

The lords of the manors at once pleaded that such a claim was not possible, but their plea was rejected. They then turned to the Court of Appeal, but failed there also. Undeterred, they went before the House of Lords to argue that the inquiry of the Royal Commission ought not to be pre-empted by a court case. The House of Lords ruled that, on the contrary, it would actually assist the Commission if the case were to be heard. During three years' detailed preparation of the Corporation's case, Bob Hunter was given the additional task of instructing Counsel and selecting witnesses to appear before the Commissioners. On 29 June 1874 the case of the Commissioners of Sewers v. Glasse and Others opened before Judge Jessel, Master of the Rolls. The hearing lasted for 22 days. Dorothy Hunter describes the scene, in which her father directed operations from behind a screen of assisting lawyers:

> The great interests at issue were defended on either side by some of the most eminent men then practising at the Bar. A reporter present on the first day wrote that owing to 'the exceptional nature of Counsel's brief, comprising as it does huge volumes of proceedings in the forestal and manorial courts from earliest times, the customary blue bag has been perforce discarded in favour of a series of large tin boxes, which render entrance to the well of the court an undertaking of some difficulty.'[17] Among the many impressive documents cited by Counsel in his opening address was a whole series of claims, established before the highest Forest Court in the reign of Charles I in which the Lords and Ladies of the Manors claimed with one accord, among other rights and privileges, a right of pasture for themselves and their men and tenants of their Manors in the waste and commonable places of the Forest: the very right now claimed by the City. 'At all events', commented the Judge, 'you have not invented this for the first time.' It was

also proved by records covering six centuries that the right of pasture had always been regulated by the Forest Courts and not by the Manor Courts. Records of the 18th century showed that all horses and cattle turned out on the Forest were required to be marked, that a local officer called a 'reeve' was appointed in each parish to see to the marking of the cattle, to make returns of the number of beasts marked, to impound unmarked beasts found in the Forest and to see that all cattle were driven home before the fence month. That these regulations were observed well into the nineteenth century was proved by the testimony of between seventy and eighty living witnesses.[18]

Bob Hunter had scoured the Forest for his witnesses: old men and women who could speak from experience of the customs prevailing in their youth. He produced three men who had once held the office of reeve, described by a patronising reporter as 'venerable individuals with white hair, tottering gait and a remarkable density of deafness'. Nevertheless they gave a clear account of their former duties, as did other witnesses who had assisted them, and the children of commoners who had once looked after their parents' livestock. To his delight these witnesses without exception proved resilient under cross-examination and told their story plainly: the Forest brand mark on commoners' cattle was a crown, accompanied by a letter, which denoted the parish from which the beast came. No animal bearing these marks could be excluded from any part of the Forest.

By contrast, the bailiffs, estate managers and farmers called as witnesses for the defence frequently contradicted their own sworn affidavits, and told half-truths:

Men who had stated that cattle could be pounded for straying on any other manor than the one where they belonged and that their own cattle had been so pounded, when questioned admitted that their cattle were pounded because they were on the roads or because they were not marked. A witness who had stated that in consequence of notice from the reeve he had had to fetch back his cattle that had strayed onto other manors, when asked by the Judge if he was compelled to fetch them back, said 'No'. He was told by the reeve where his cattle were in case he should want them nearer home: the reeves of the different parishes communicated with each other: 'That', explained the witness, 'was the way we found our things.'[19]

Towards the close of the trial, Judge Jessel began to display noticeable impatience with the defendants. His judgement was that the plaintiffs were entitled to an injunction restraining further enclosures and that all lands enclosed since 14 August 1851, the date of the government's last legal enclosure, were to be thrown open again, with the exception of those already built on or turned into graveyards or gardens. He did not wish, he said, 'the enormous inconvenience of ordering the wholesale demolition of houses and churches'.[20] Awarding costs to the plaintiffs, the Judge accused the defendants of endeavouring to support their title by 'a vast bulk of false evidence'.[21] He ended by praising Bob Hunter's work in the case.

Several months after the court hearing, in March 1875, the Royal Commission issued its first Report. It had met for 102 days, examined 139 witnesses, amassed a great pile of evidence and, to no one's surprise, had reached virtually the same conclusion as the Rolls Court. To be doubly certain of its hold on Epping Forest, the Corporation of London now began buying rights from the lords of the manors, the value of which had been drastically reduced by Jessel's verdict. Ironically, they then proceeded to resist the commoners' claims for compensation.

In 1878, under Disraeli's government, an Act vested control and maintenance of Epping Forest in the Corporation, and directed that no buildings should ever be erected upon it: the Forest should remain open for all time. The office of Verderer was revived and, by commission of the Queen, a Ranger was appointed to give effect to Forest bye-laws. Bob Hunter was engaged in wresting maximum benefit for the Corporation from the arbitration which settled the boundaries. 'Never in the past experience of the Law Courts', according to Shaw-Lefevre, 'was there a decision by which upwards of four hundred persons were compelled to disgorge three thousand acres of land wrongfully enclosed.'[22]

The CPS succeeded in inserting a clause into the new Act which directed the Arbitrator, Lord Hobhouse, to compensate the inhabitants of Loughton for the loss of their lopping rights. On the eve of Martinmas 1879, the traditional onset of winter, an estimated 5,000 people turned out by torchlight to indulge their last opportunity of swinging an axe on Epping Forest. Only commoners were supposed to have this privilege, but on this occasion, no one was refused. In compensation for their loss, cottagers who had once exercised their rights were paid £1,000 in all. A further £6,000 was given for the benefit of all the inhabitants of Loughton, to erect a parish meeting room to be called the 'Loppers Hall'. As Shaw-Lefevre observed:

The sequel to this award had a most humorous aspect. The day came, some two years later, when the foundation-stone of this village hall was to be laid, and it was made the occasion of a popular demonstration at Loughton. With singular infelicity, the local managers responsible for it invited the Lord Mayor of London to perform this ceremony, unmindful of the fact that the Corporation of London had done their very utmost to defeat the claim of the inhabitants to any compensation for their rights. The Lord Mayor drove down in state to Loughton. The proceedings were there opened with a prayer by Mr. Maitland, the Rector of the parish, and Lord of the Manor, who had done his utmost to inclose the whole of the waste of his Manor, and to defeat the claim of the inhabitants of Loughton.[23]

The local managers at least had the good taste not to invite any members of the CPS to take part in the proceedings in such company.

In May 1882 Queen Victoria herself, in the company of Princesses Beatrice and Louise, rode through Chingford in an open carriage, with policemen and guardsmen lining the route, to High Beech. Here she dedicated Epping Forest 'to the use and enjoyment of the public for all time'.[24]

Bob Hunter's conduct of the Epping Forest trial and other CPS cases involved him in work which occupied most of his waking hours. In January 1872, scarcely three years after his marriage, his wife Emily died, in the advanced stages of her first pregnancy. Following this tragedy the CPS and the great court case occupied the whole of his life.

In 1874 he was advising on an agreement for the conservation of more than 300 acres of Dartford Heath. Two years later he was aiding a local branch of the CPS to fight for the 1,300 acres of Banstead Common, high land on the North Surrey Downs commanding some of the finest views of the Thames Valley and the Weald of Surrey and Sussex. With his support, the case fought for Ashdown Forest was won on appeal in 1881.

Amongst the many heaths and woodlands which were systematically protected after Epping, there was one inquiry which turned out to be of equal importance. The New Forest had been designated a Royal hunting ground by William the Conqueror, and the history of its management was not dissimilar to that of Epping. The dock of the Verderers' Court at Lyndhurst, a crude black-oak perch set opposite the bench of Forest Justice, today gives some idea of the setting in which offenders against Forest laws were once arraigned and sentenced.

For centuries the woods of the New Forest were kept stocked with deer, and planted for military purposes with beech, fir and oak. In the naval dockyard at Buckler's Hard on the Beaulieu River, sloops, frigates and battleships, including Nelson's *Agamemnon*, were built entirely of local timber. A 74-gun vessel no more than 30 months on the slipway could require the felling of some 2,000 trees.[25] In the eighteenth and early nineteenth centuries large portions of the Forest were fenced off to protect nurseries of saplings grown for this purpose, but the common rights were never seriously infringed. It was a proud boast of the smallholders, both tenants and cottagers, that they so enjoyed their rights as to have no need of the Poor Laws.

All this took place before the Office of Woods and Forests, by the Deer Removal Act of 1851, began the process of converting 65,000 acres into a single-species woodland. The variety of vegetation and natural harvests began rapidly to disappear as row upon row of fir trees for the production of softwood were planted. This policy went on unchecked for more than two decades.

It was not until 1871 that Fawcett succeeded in getting a motion passed in the House of Commons preventing all felling and new enclosures pending the drawing up of a new Act. A Select Committee was appointed, to whom the interests of commoners and the general public in the Forest were represented under the guidance of Bob Hunter. He worked closely with local residents, who had formed the New Forest Association. Broader in scope than that for Epping, the evidence he presented was required not so much as proof of common rights, as to establish that the Forest was something more than a timber factory. His witnesses were widely drawn: from landowner, barrister, local surveyor and land valuer, to small farmer and labourer, each chosen to explain the particular ways in which common rights maintained the social fabric. The opinions of a naturalist and a local historian were also introduced. As a result, in 1877 the New Forest was brought under an Act of Parliament framed specifically to preserve its natural aspects, and a new Court of Verderers elected. Enclosure schemes for commons on the edge of the Forest were opposed in the law courts and successfully defeated; existing timber enclosures were frozen. Today the entire Forest is the most extensive area of semi-natural vegetation in lowland Britain. Like Epping Forest, it is designated an area of Special Scientific Interest because of its importance as a habitat for wildlife.

Bob Hunter remarried in 1877, and his second wife Ellen bore him three daughters. Three years later he bought Meadfields, a large house in the village of Haslemere in Surrey where he was to live for the next 32 years. He took an active part in local life, being chairman of the Parish Council and speaking frequently at meetings on education and temperance reform. 'As a speaker he was admirably clear and direct, articulate but not rhetorical, relying far more on the persuasive force of exact statement than on appeals to emotion … No one ever appealed to him in vain for advice in a local difficulty.'[26]

In 1882 he relinquished his position with the CPS and became Chief Solicitor to the Post Office during Fawcett's term of office as Postmaster General. Bob Hunter's skill in drawing up Acts of Parliament for the Post Office was equal to that of the Treasury Department's own draughtsmen, who normally dealt with such matters. It was estimated that he saved ten million pounds in negotiating the Conveyance of Mails Act and greatly improved the efficiency of the Post Office Savings Bank. 'He made it his rule to form his own conclusions and to give his own advice instead of relying on opinion obtained from outside.'[27]

Although no longer on the staff of the CPS, he remained closely connected with the Society, of which he became vice-chairman, and he was also chairman of the Kent and Surrey Footpaths Committee. 1896 saw the publication of Bob Hunter's *Open Spaces, Footpaths and Rights of Way*. The distillation of a lifetime's experience of the legalities of open-air leisure rights, this book was a bible for the CPS local committees, rambling clubs and parish councils. It is a model of clarity, easily understood by the layman, yet leaving no aspect of the law unexamined.

As well as continuing to advise the CPS and later starting the process which would bring the National Trust into existence, Bob Hunter for many years acted as chairman of the Hampstead Garden Suburb Trust and the Metropolitan Public Gardens Association. He was also appointed President of the first Federation of Rambling Clubs, the precursor of the Ramblers' Association. In recognition of his services to the open space movement, he was knighted in 1894.

CHAPTER 3

Octavia Hill

In the early part of the nineteenth century, Wisbech was a small and prosperous town surrounded by orchards; a busy inland port on the River Nene. Here, in a fine Queen Anne house, once the home of the High Sheriff of Cambridgeshire, James Hill was engaged in the banking, corn and wool trade which had been founded by his father. Octavia, his eighth child, was born on 3 December 1838. She was the third daughter of his marriage to Caroline Southwood Smith, a schoolteacher with advanced views on education, on which she had published several articles.

Both Caroline and her husband were Unitarians; Christians who reject the doctrines of the Trinity and of original sin, believing instead in the unity of God and the innate goodness of humanity. They identified themselves with numerous liberal and progressive causes. Among his many and varied activities James Hill had opened a theatre in Wisbech, launched a Radical penny newspaper, and was personally responsible for founding one of the first primary schools in England. Convinced of the sanctity of human life, he once rode 40 miles to Cambridge Assizes to plead successfully for a reprieve for the last man in England sentenced to hang for sheep-stealing. His optimistic belief in human nature was of little avail, however, when, during one of the country's recurrent financial crises, he was unable to meet demands on his bank and in 1840 was declared bankrupt.

For the sake of economy the children of James Hill's two previous marriages were put into the care of their maternal grandparents, the Queen Anne house was given up and the family left Wisbech, never to return. This upheaval undermined Octavia's feeling of security and affected her behaviour. At times she was excessively boisterous, at other times completely withdrawn. She would not play with a dolls' house, which perhaps reminded her of the house in Wisbech, and when asked to say what she did want, replied a field 'so large that I could run in it for ever'.[1]

Caroline refused to talk about the catastrophe, not wishing to upset her children, but the result of her reticence was the opposite of what she intended. Octavia gained the impression that her family's lack of means was an unmentionable shame, and that they were all somehow responsible. Consequently, she began to hate all luxury and ostentation and embarked upon a life committed to the virtues of frugality and economy. She dressed simply, preferred plain food and invariably travelled either third class or on foot. She would one day handle charitable funds worth thousands of pounds for the National Trust and other organisations, the donors always confident that not a penny would be misspent.

From Wisbech they moved to Epping, the children afterwards recalling many a long walk in the Forest. Then to Hampstead, Gloucester, Leeds and once more to the vicinity of London as James tried again but failed to re-establish himself in business. Finally he suffered a complete mental breakdown and was no longer able to work.

By the time Octavia reached adolescence, Caroline was of necessity the dominant parent. The family home by then was a small cottage in Finchley, still a rural village. The girls so often played outside, in all weathers, that they became known locally as 'the young ladies who are always up in the hedges'.[2]

Caroline's father was now supporting the family financially and Octavia spent a great deal of time with him, walking from Finchley to visit him at his home on the edge of Hampstead Heath, near Kenwood. Dr Southwood Smith had at one time been a Unitarian minister, but later took up a career in medicine. He worked as a doctor in the Fever Hospital in East London, and there he was made acutely aware that the principal causes of epidemic were not contagion, but slum housing, overcrowding, poor sanitation and a lack of clean water and open spaces. He campaigned vigorously for reforms which were eventually embodied in the first Public Health Act of 1848. Octavia helped him to copy out extracts of medical reports and legislation, which made her aware for the first time of the appalling poverty which existed in the cities of Victorian England.

In 1851 Caroline accepted the management of the Co-operative Guild, a combination of school and craft workshop for women. Conducted along the lines of a 'mission to the poor' and financed by a committee of wealthy evangelicals and Christian Socialists, the Guild was housed in a large, gloomy building at the back of Fitzroy Square, where the Hills now made their home. The appointment of Caroline, a Unitarian, seemed at first to be a victory for the Christian Socialists, represented by Vansittart Neale, who laid stress on social reform rather than religious conversion as a means of helping the poor. The Hill family became friends and admirers of Neale and his associates, among them the author Charles Kingsley and the Reverend Frederick Denison Maurice. Meetings addressed by these eloquent idealists were invariably attended by Caroline and her daughters, and every morning Octavia, accompanied by her elder sister Miranda, went to the service conducted by Maurice at Lincoln's Inn Chapel. On the way home she would walk alongside Maurice bombarding him with questions about Christian doctrine, and under his influence she soon abandoned Unitarianism and became a confirmed member of the Church of England.

Loss of the Finchley countryside plunged Octavia into melancholy and her state of mind was not helped by reading graphic descriptions of the effects of urban poverty in Henry Mayhew's *London Labour and the London Poor*. Her mother's remedy was a form of shock treatment. She decided that the best thing for her daughter, still only 14, was to give her charge of more than 20 Ragged School girls, some considerably older than herself, who earned a small wage at the Guild by manufacturing toys for the children of the well-to-do. The stark reality behind Dr Southwood Smith's health reports was now brought home to Octavia. She saw for herself the effects of chronic disease, malnutrition, exhaustion and physical abuse. Fiercely indignant at the plight of her toy workers, she threw herself into a frenzy of activity on their behalf. As well as teaching them how to read and write and managing the production and sale of the toys, she organised a midday meal for her workers, visited them when they were sick, and at weekends arranged nature-study walks on the London commons. Octavia's sister Gertrude describes how she was once out on Highgate Lane listening to a professor discoursing on mosses. Octavia suddenly 'leapt down from the bank with a staff in her hand, a straw hat on her head, torn by the thicket, followed by a troop of ragged toymakers, happy and flushed, each with an armful of bluebells'.[3]

These activities did not meet with everyone's approval. Putting the interests of her workers first, Octavia often made arrangements for them without first informing the Guild's management committee. Things finally came to a head when in 1853 she invited Maurice to teach the weekly scripture lesson in the toy workshop. He had just been dismissed from his professorship at King's College for criticising some aspects of orthodox Christian doctrine, and Neale and the committee, disapproving of Octavia's lack of consultation, rescinded the invitation. Caroline resigned over the affront to Maurice, and following her departure the Guild went into irreversible decline. Her daughters stayed on until it was wound up three years later.

Octavia was then offered work as a secretary in the Christian Socialists' Women's College in Great Ormond Street and over the next few years made many new acquaintances. In 1860 she met Sophia Jex-Blake, who was to pioneer the acceptance of women into the medical profession. They went on holiday together to North Wales and Sophia lived with the Hills until unbearable friction between herself and Caroline forced Octavia to choose between friendship, and loyalty to her family. The family came first, and Sophia had to leave. About the same time, another friend, Mary Harris, introduced Octavia to the joys of fell-walking in the Lake District, where she worked for a time as a nanny. In the winter of 1863 Octavia was employed in London, teaching the children of Tom Hughes MP, and later canvassed for him in his unsuccessful campaign to win the constituency of Marylebone for the Liberals. She was also a friend and admirer of John Ruskin, the famous author of *Modern Painters*, whom she first met when he visited the Guild in search of examples of new craft work.

Then in his mid-thirties, Ruskin had already achieved considerable notoriety. The failure of his marriage had caused a scandal, but he had attracted even more public opprobrium by his enthusiastic support of the artists known as the 'pre-Raphaelite Brotherhood'. Octavia, who was less than half his age, was to discover that Ruskin could be charming and sociable. In response to her request for art training he invited her to visit him at his home on Denmark Hill, where she found his study walls crammed with Turner's paintings. She could not help but comment on the beauty of her surroundings and was then confronted for the first but by no means the last time with Ruskin's deep pessimism: 'He answered that if I could change places with him, I should be no happier than I am now. I said I knew that very well; but I affirmed there was a positive pleasure in a beautiful thing.'[4]

For the next nine years, in addition to her other employment, Octavia spent up to six hours every day copying the great masters under Ruskin's supervision, in galleries where he was also at work. His insistence on exactitude crushed her creativity. When she asked 'whether and how I should try to set down in drawing any of the gloriously wonderful things I see, day after day, in the streets and everywhere, but which depend on expression' he discouraged her. 'If you devote yourself to human expression, I know how it will be, you will watch more and more, and there will be an end of art for you. You will say "*Hang* drawing!! I must go to help people." '[5]

Ruskin was expressing a longing which he himself was eventually to share with Octavia. They had much in common, not least that unhappy feature of home life, the stern and oppressive mother. They both suffered from severe depression at times and turned to thoughts of the countryside for solace. In her love of art and architecture Octavia shared his predilections, gaining a heightened awareness of the beauty of old vernacular buildings and wild landscapes.

Just at the time when she was receiving some well-paid commissions for portraiture and was beginning to make her own mark as an artist, it was Ruskin, ironically, who gave Octavia the opportunity to indulge her social concerns. He had first hinted at having changed his mind about her future career during a party they attended at the home of Burne-Jones. A year later, in 1864, he offered her loans from the fortune he had inherited from his father, to enable her to go out and do whatever she thought best to improve the living conditions of the poor. She accepted the offer, and with the money bought three houses in Paradise Place, among the most dilapidated properties in Marylebone. This purchase marked the beginning of the extensive housing improvement schemes for which Octavia Hill is best remembered.

Within a few months she was transforming her property. She could be seen, with a bunch of rusty keys in one hand and a newspaper-wrapped rent box under her arm, making her way purposefully through suffocating rooms piled high with the blackened rubbish of ages. After her trailed builder, surveyor, sweep and broker. She rejoiced in her power to be able to say 'Break out a window there in that dark corner; let God's light and air in', or 'Trap that foul drain, and shut the poisonous miasma out.'[6] Overcrowded, damp and filthy rooms were cleared, dried, renovated and re-let to their former occupants under strict rules banning subletting. The rents were collected personally by Octavia in order to ensure that these rules were adhered to, and she would not listen to any excuses for non-payment. Necessary repairs were swiftly carried out, and the tenants were given rebates if they kept their homes in good order. Wherever there was even a small open space forming part of the property, it was cleared and made into a children's playground, or, with the aid of Ruskin's gardener, replanted with flowers and shrubs for the enjoyment of her tenants.

At Freshwater Place she bought a row of run-down cottages facing a small triangle of ground, covered with stagnant puddles and heaps of rubbish, where the residents kept a few hens, rabbits and doves. This insanitary but no doubt well-loved urban farmyard was cleared, drained, paved and enclosed, and converted into a supervised playground, but not without resistance. Bricks were stolen, rubbish thrown back, workmen threatened and the railings demolished. In spite of confessing to a sense of 'bitter hopelessness', Octavia persevered, and eventually the completed playground was successfully inaugurated, with maypole and flags and the band from a Boys' Home. Some 70 children went home from the party with bunches of flowers, an orange and a piece of cake. Later, in a letter to Mary Harris, Octavia described a day as playground supervisor:

> Yesterday I set all the children to make small flags out of old bright coloured stuff, and cut out the letters of their names for them to sew on; their joy was intense; hour after hour passed, and they seemed never to weary. Then I hired an organ man to come in, and the children's joy was overflowing. The whole ground was covered with tiny dancing figures; each child danced alone a step rather like a jig; if you could but have seen the beaming smiles ...[7]

The playground was open during the summer months after school and all day on Saturdays. A week's admission ticket cost a penny for each child. In the daytime, women were allowed to use the area to hang out their washing. It was for its time perhaps the city's most intensively used small open space.

Octavia's housing renovation schemes soon became widely known, and offers to finance them poured in. By the 1870s, she was finding it necessary to train other women to help her. They became the first 'social workers' in the modern sense, concerned for the total welfare of families in their homes.

A steady return on investment was achieved, but Octavia's system did not escape criticism. She was attacked for making scapegoats of tenants who were labelled irredeemably 'bad characters'. As an example to others, consistent defaulters were evicted and, following the principles of the recently founded Charity Organisation Society, she put a stop to the doles which, according to her philosophy, sapped the recipients' will to work. Ruskin now had doubts about the capitalist basis of the schemes which he had helped to finance. He strongly objected to a paper entitled 'The Importance of Aiding the Poor without Almsgiving' which Octavia read to the Social Science Association. She was not taking into account the inadequacy of wage levels which were the root cause of poverty.

When the Charity Organisation Society commissioned a full-scale enquiry into housing for the working classes, Octavia was appointed to its committee. Other members included Tom Hughes, Sydney Waterlow, who was the founder of an Industrial Dwellings Company, and Baroness Burdett-Coutts, a pioneer of model tenements and the idea of a 'garden city'. The COS Report appeared almost at the same time as a collection of Octavia's articles and papers entitled *Homes of the London Poor*. These two publications materially affected the course of new legislation under the Conservative government, and Octavia now found herself in regular consultation with the Home Secretary, Richard Cross. Henceforward local authorities were to be given powers of compulsory purchase so that they might put into effect their own housing schemes. By the time the Artisans' Dwellings Act came onto the Statute Book early in 1875, the small, impatient, somewhat humourless woman, who was judged to be a true successor of her grandfather, had made her mark as a reformer.

In the same year as the enactment of the Artisans' Dwellings Act, Octavia turned her attention to the issue of urban open spaces. Her housing schemes were now sufficiently well established to allow her to look at the wider issues of urban planning. Swiss Cottage Fields and the meadows below Parliament Hill had until that time formed the northern boundary of the metropolis, and their preservation seemed vital. She discovered that they had been sold to a builder. Rights of way existed over these fields, which were used by Sunday walkers, but there were no rights of common. Having played there as a child when she lived at Finchley, the beauty of the pastures, hedgerows and trees was indelibly fixed in her memory.

To obtain advice on how she might try to save the fields, Octavia consulted the Commons Preservation Society, where she met Bob Hunter for the first time. He confirmed her supposition that the only hope of preserving such a large, privately-owned open space would be to persuade a public benefactor to purchase the land. She immediately went to see the contractor, and after the interview was satisfied that if she could raise 10,000 guineas, he would be willing to sell.

She first approached Ruskin for the money, but was unable any longer to enlist his support. Counting on her influence as a well-known public figure, she put out an appeal through the columns of *The Times*, and in barely three weeks had raised £9,500, when suddenly, the flood of donations was reduced to a trickle. It was early August. The patrons of good causes had by now gone on holiday. The target figure was nearly reached, however, and Octavia felt the matter was secure enough to allow her to take a few days rest with some friends in Gloucestershire.

She was unaware that the owner of the land had taken it for granted that her idea was a pipe-dream, and that the start of building would not be seriously delayed. Alarmed to discover from the published list of subscribers that the total had in fact nearly been raised, he withdrew his offer at five days' notice. The battle was lost. Fitzjohn's Avenue and the villas of a prosperous housing estate now cover the fields. 'I cannot tell you', wrote Octavia to her supporters, 'how terrible to me appear the vast spaces of ground covered with houses inhabited by persons at one dead level of poverty; sometimes the tracts appropriated to the houses of the wealthy seem to me in another way more terrible.'[8]

The seeds of disaffection between herself and Ruskin, which prevented her from securing an immediate loan for the fields, had sadly been sown by Octavia herself, even before her lecture to the Social Science Association. At the height of his generosity towards her housing schemes, in a letter to Mary Harris, she had once compared Ruskin's character unfavourably with that of the artist G. F. Watts, a 'transparently, deeply good, a quiet sympathetic man, with large childlike heart ... There is nothing pathetic about Watts, as there is about Ruskin.'[9] The rift, then, was slowly to develop over differences of ideology, until Ruskin no longer felt bound to respond to the evils of the urban social crisis by supporting every one of Octavia's good causes. He now spent most of his time at Brantwood, his new home in the Lake District. His reply to the Swiss Cottage fields appeal confirmed Octavia's opinion that as far as cities were concerned, he was irredeemably pessimistic:

I cannot help in this more than with sympathy and good hope. There is no reason for you doubting either of these in me, for all you have done and are designing – but my work is now, and must be totally in another kind; not as you put it, that I want perfection, while you are content with the immediate possible – but that while your work is only mitigating of mortal pain, mine is radically curative – London is as utterly doomed as

Gomorrah, that is no reason why you should not open a window, or bring a field to give a moment longer breath to her plague-stricken children, but I have to labour wholly to fence round fresh fields beyond the smoke of her torment. I would fain have helped you to get these (Swiss Cottage) fields, because of your own personal love of them, but in many ways, at present, I am helpless.[10]

The fresh fields to which Ruskin refers were his plans for cooperatives and artistic enterprises to be run by the Guild of St George of which he was the founder and self-appointed 'Master'. It was a grand conception, but in practice its achievements were limited. Reproductions of Italian art were financed by the Guild, and displayed, alongside mineral specimens and manuscripts, in a small museum in Sheffield. Land, including 20 acres of copsewood at Bewdley, and a small field in Derbyshire, was accepted on the Guild's behalf for cultivation and recreation. Yet, despite Ruskin, an important outcome of the unsuccessful bid to save Swiss Cottage fields was that Octavia joined the CPS, and within a few months found herself involved in a fierce parliamentary battle over the future of common land.

In the Queen's Speech of February 1876, the Tory administration led by Disraeli declared its intention of unlocking the shackles with which Fawcett had effectively constrained the Inclosure Commissioners. Two days later, the Home Secretary, who had until that time been Octavia's friend and supporter, presented to the House of Commons a Bill for 'facilitating the regulation and improvement of commons, and for the amendment of the Inclosure Acts', a title which naturally aroused the suspicions of the CPS lobby, most of whom were now on the Opposition benches. It appeared from the contents of the draft that the enclosure machine was to be set in motion again but with greater efficiency. In the debate on the Second Reading, Shaw-Lefevre introduced an amendment: 'No enclosures should be permitted except under the special sanction of Parliament.'[11] If passed, this would effectively wreck the Bill.

Arguments for and against the amendment were on predictable lines until an enthusiastic Tory backbencher expressed his satisfaction that if the Bill were to become law it might dispel the unacceptable notion that the inhabitants of large towns had a right to wander over distant commons as they pleased. His sentiments caused an uproar, for they were quite out of keeping with the tenor of the Home Secretary's speeches. Fawcett at once seized his opportunity, calling upon Richard Cross to disavow immediately the interpretation being put upon his Bill. What remained of the common lands was surely 'a great and valuable possession to be enjoyed ... by the people of the entire country, who liked to wander to those commons to see beautiful scenery or seek for recreation, health and fresh air'.

As might have been expected, Cross vigorously denied that his proposed statute would decrease access to the countryside. He now argued that the whole purpose of his legislation

> was, as far as possible, to prevent the enclosure of commons
> and to give facilities for keeping them open for the benefit
> of the people; so that not only those who had rights of
> common should enjoy them, but that the public themselves
> might enjoy the use of those free spaces of land, improved,
> drained and levelled.[12]

He concluded by quoting a well-worn epigram:

> The law condemns the man and woman
> Who steals a goose from off the common;
> But lets the greater felon loose,
> Who steals the common from the goose.

'He had no intention', he declared, 'of stealing the common from any goose, but to afford every possible facility for the continued use by the poor artisan and dwellers in great towns of all that beautiful scenery they had hitherto enjoyed, but in an improved state.'[13]

In the light of this assurance, Shaw-Lefevre and Fawcett withdrew their amendment, to gain time to publicise the discrepancy between the Home Secretary's declared intentions, and the wide-ranging scope of the Bill. Cross neither admitted that his Bill had any inadequacies – not the least of which being that it seemed merely to amend the Act of 1845 – nor expressed any intention of altering its provisions to suit his opponents. The period between the Second and Third Readings was crucial if the CPS was to mobilise public opinion against the proposed legislation.

Octavia proved a valuable ally of the CPS in its campaign outside Parliament. When Richard Cross had consulted her about the Artisans' Dwellings Bill, there had been a danger of Fawcett attacking some of its provisions. She therefore sought a meeting with Fawcett, to discuss his possible objections. She knew how effective an opponent he could be, and that his wife Millicent was a leading advocate of women's suffrage, with which Octavia had no sympathy.

At that first meeting, her anxieties were soon allayed. Octavia won Fawcett over to her views on housing and was now, a year later, willing to side wholeheartedly with him against the Commons Bill. They agreed that she should write a forceful article on the subject, that he should co-ordinate farm labourers' petitions, and that Bob Hunter and Shaw-Lefevre between them should write a critique, to appear in the forthcoming CPS Report.

Six weeks later, Octavia's article was published in *Macmillan's Magazine*; its tone was unmistakably one of forthright attack. She began with a dramatic description of the effects of the 1871 Bank Holiday Act which gave millions of working people a day off, of which many took advantage to visit the countryside. She foresaw a considerable loss of rural open space for public enjoyment should the Inclosure Commissioners be given a free hand with agricultural improvement schemes. Landowners and titleholders were taken to task for the way in which they patronised farm labourers and took from them the heritage of their common lands:

> Should we stand by, we who ought to see farther, and let
> them part with what ought to be a possession to the many
> in the future? A few coals at Christmas, which rapidly come
> to be looked upon as a charity graciously accorded by the
> rich, or the recipients of which are arbitrarily selected by
> them, may in many cases be blindly accepted by cottagers
> in lieu of Common rights ... Do not let us deceive ourselves
> as to the result of this Bill if it pass unamended.[14]

That the government was infuriated by Octavia's part in the CPS propaganda campaign became evident in the debate in the House of Commons which took place before the Bill went into the Committee stage. By then Conservative Associations up and down the country had been badgered to start a petition in support of the revived enclosure procedures. Richard Cross charged the CPS with factiousness and with deliberately misrepresenting his proposals. Fawcett was now pressing an amendment stating in no uncertain terms that farm workers and the general public were not being served by the government. So fierce were the accusations flying across the floor of the House that the late-night sitting ended in almost total disarray. Confused and befuddled MPs entered the division lobbies four times before the Bill was allowed to proceed.

The CPS kept up the pressure during the Committee stage of the Bill, even though, as a minority, they were not in a position to force substantial alterations. The writer Leslie Stephen, leader of the

Sunday Tramps walking club and an observer of the protracted proceedings in Parliament that year, identified the CPS stalwarts as Fawcett, Shaw-Lefevre, Sir Charles Dilke, Sir William Harcourt, Francis Cowper-Temple and Lord Edmond Fitzmaurice. He recorded with some bitterness that 'no ex-Cabinet Minister took any share in a work not unworthy of the exertions of the Liberal Party'.[15] It seemed that the 'right' to enclose was once more sacrosanct. No proportion of land for purposes of recreation was guaranteed; commons near large towns and cities were to remain almost as vulnerable as those elsewhere in the kingdom; opposition to non-statutory enclosures would remain as difficult and as expensive as ever; encroachers would incur no other penalty than the possibility of losing what was not theirs in the first place.

The Bill became law on 11 August, and whilst at the time its almost unscathed appearance on the Statute Book seemed a major defeat for the open space movement, it nevertheless gradually became clear that the actual working of the legislation was not to prove as detrimental to the public interest as the CPS had at first feared. The force with which the Society had put forward its case changed the collective attitude of the Inclosure Commissioners. This showed clearly in their handling of specific proposals. A total of 38 applications for enclosure which had been awaiting approval by the Home Secretary were sent back to the Commissioners for re-examination in the light of the new legislation, and of these no less than 18 were turned down on the grounds that 'it was not proved to their satisfaction that it was for the benefit of the neighbourhood'.[16]

All the Commission's recommendations were now scrutinised by a Select Committee which included William Harcourt and Henry Fawcett. The long-term effect of their influence was considerable. Whereas during the ten years from 1859 to 1869 approximately 260,000 acres of common land were legally enclosed, in the 20 years following the end of the CPS campaign fought with Octavia's help, this figure was reduced to less than 26,000 acres. After 1896 requests for regulation were almost the only applications received. 'Practically', Bob Hunter wrote in 1897, the Commissioners' 'proposals have lately been confined to common fields and to large tracts of waste in mountain districts, and, even in the latter case, they have required the insertion of a provision that the access of the public shall not be interfered with, unless the lands are actually brought into tillage or put under cultivation.'[17]

The campaign to protect common land continues to this day. Enclosure is still a threat, especially in upland areas, although it is fiercely resisted by the Open Spaces Society, the successor to the CPS.

The year following the debate over the new Commons Act was the most difficult period of Octavia's life. A combination of circumstances reduced her to a state of nervous collapse. She had been deeply upset by the death of her close friend Janie Hughes, who had been voluntary secretary of the housing schemes. Her secret engagement to Edward Bond, a barrister whom she had met during her efforts to save Swiss Cottage fields, had been broken off, and she had become embroiled in an intractable dispute over the future of the disused Quaker burial ground at Bunhill Fields in East London. The final blow was a bitter quarrel with Ruskin, culminating in his publication of their recent exchange of letters, which she had specifically requested should remain private.

Octavia was once more in the grip of the same difficulties which had clouded her childhood and adolescence, and by August she was obliged to give up work. She was too frightened to see anyone. 'I feel as if eyes and eyes and eyes had been on me for months, and my own never closed.'[18]

Her sanity was saved by the intervention of Harriot Yorke. A calm and capable woman of her own age, Harriot had at first been merely a polite acquaintance; a well-to-do subscriber to Octavia's good causes. In this period of crisis, however, she quickly became an invaluable friend, taking over the awkward decisions of Octavia's public life and organising her affairs with great tact, until Octavia recovered her health and her will to work again. A seasoned traveller and woman of means, Harriot decided that Octavia needed a long holiday. She arranged for them both to spend several weeks in Italy and Switzerland. Regaining some of her old confidence, Octavia took up sketching once more.

As she slowly regained her strength on her return, Octavia applied her mind once again to the needs of her housing tenants, and the provision of public open spaces. The article written in response to the 1876 Commons Bill had declared that access to the countryside was essential for the well-being of all people living and working in the urban and industrial environment. Her espousal of the freedom of nature in contrast to the oppressive life of the city, while partly the outcome of her contact with the spirit of Romanticism in nineteenth-century art through her association with Ruskin, was none the less more deeply motivated by her unhappy experiences in childhood and adolescence. Fitzroy Square's gloomy atmosphere had left an indelible impression on her memory. Because of the circumstances of her father's breakdown she could not face the angst associated with intimate relationships. Contemplation of natural beauty alone gratified her intense longing for peace.

> Sometimes on a hot summer evening ... when I am trying to
> calm excited women shouting their execrable language at one
> another, I have looked up suddenly and seen one of those bright
> gleams of light the summer sun sends out just before he sets,
> catching the top of a red chimney pot, and beautiful there,
> though too directly above their heads for the crowd below to
> notice it much. But to me it brings sad thoughts of the fair and
> quiet places far away, where it is falling softly on tree, and hill,
> and cloud and I feel as if that quiet, that beauty, that space,
> would be more powerful to calm the wild excess about me
> than all my frantic striving with it.[19]

In a speech to the National Health Society before her breakdown,
referring to the countryside, made more accessible by the construction of railways, she appealed to her audience to

> keep those fair, far, still places for your children, and your
> children's children, if you can: the more cities increase, the
> more precious they will be; for the more man's soul will long
> for the beauty, for the quiet, which the city does not, cannot,
> give.[20]

Octavia was acutely aware, nevertheless, that the countryside
was, for most of the tenants of her housing schemes, a world far
removed from their experience. She had instigated the endeavour to
save Swiss Cottage fields not for the wealthy residents of Hampstead, but for the poor of Lisson Grove. There had been much talk by
politicians, but only limited action on provision of open space, especially in North and East London, and other heavily built-up areas.

The uneven distribution of what used to be called 'pleasure
gardens' had for some time been an embarrassment to the reform-
ing pride of municipal authorities. Whereas fashionable town resi-
dences of the eighteenth century were built round private squares
and crescents, there was no such pleasance in the early nineteenth
century for the enjoyment of the poor. The fine Crown Parks were
nearly all on the west side of London, for the benefit of royalty, the
aristocracy and the well-to-do.

Such visible evidence of social inequality in the city, and the
dearth of open spaces in the industrial centres of the North and
Midlands, had prompted the setting up in 1833 (the year after the
Reform Bill) of a Select Committee on Public Walks.[21] This Com-

mittee suggested the establishment and maintenance by voluntary, local authority or central government funding, of open spaces in or near areas occupied by the working classes. Walking in the open air would be infinitely preferable to drinking, dog-fights and boxing matches; health, attitudes to work and productivity would all be greatly improved.

There was no sudden rush to create open spaces as a result of this Report, but its recommendations were gradually put into effect. In 1845 a new 200-acre Victoria Park was opened on the outskirts of East London. It immediately became very popular and on one day alone 20,000 people were estimated to be making the most of its rather inadequate and uninspired layout. This park was a major step in the right direction, to be followed in towns and cities of the north of England and elsewhere by great improvement in access to existing botanical gardens, arboretums and pleasure grounds. Municipal authorities began to take seriously the construction of riverside, roadside and canalside walks and to plan their own public parks: Paxton's Birkenhead Park was opened in 1847; Aston Park was purchased by Birmingham Council with the aid of wealthy local philanthropists in 1864 and in the early 1870s Roundhay Park was bought by Leeds Council. In Liverpool, where the first municipal garden was built to create work for the unemployed in 1767, Newsham Park, Stanley Park and Sefton Park were all opened between 1868 and 1872. Creation of public parks became all the rage.

Commendable though these achievements were, they were always hampered by the lack of land available at a price acceptable to the ratepayers and voluntary fund-raisers. The great Public Health Act of 1875 enabled urban authorities to purchase or rent land for use as public walks or pleasure grounds, but it was Octavia Hill's belief that there was a more effective and economic way of bringing small open spaces into the public domain. Everyone had a right to be near 'the healing gift of space', so why should the reformer's answer to the lack of private gardens for poor families not be the planning of a mass of small public gardens in addition to public parks. 'Open-air sitting rooms for the poor'[22] was how she whimsically imagined them. Octavia's sister Miranda was thinking along similar lines, and it was she who first set down her thoughts in the form of an essay, which she read to the Hill family one winter evening. She proposed the formation of a 'Society for the Diffusion of Beauty'; at first sight a wildly idealistic notion, but one not impossible of at least partial fulfilment. Octavia had the essay printed, handed out amongst her friends and read to a meeting of the National Health Society, where it was received in stunned silence. The audience heard quoted the words of the Reverend Samuel Barnett, one of Octavia's former housing workers who became warden of Toynbee Hall, the university settlement in the East End. He was already under attack from some quarters for trying, it was said, to save starving souls by means of pictures, parties and pianos. Now he was heard to argue that 'the great burden of his parishioners in the East End was not poverty, but ugliness'. Miranda suggested the issue of a monthly circular with news of what was being done to beautify the poor districts of London in a variety of different ways, including small gardens.

As if to emphasise the consensus opinion that such a suggestion was too vague and impracticable to be worth further consideration, a lady in the audience stood up and expounded at length on the virtues of an inhaler; she considered it to be of far greater benefit to those with chest diseases than the beauty and air of public gardens. Octavia intervened at this point to bring the discussion back to her sister's proposals, and gradually the idea took root. The new organisation adopted a different, rather more enigmatic title than that originally suggested. It was to be known as 'The Kyrle Society', named after the philanthropist John Kyrle, the Man of Ross eulogised in Alexander Pope's *Moral Essays*, and remembered for the bequest to his native town of a modest public park.

The Kyrle Society was formally brought into being in 1878 and its Open Spaces Committee was appointed in May 1879, although by that time it had effectively been functioning for some months in all but name. Octavia was elected treasurer of the committee and Bob Hunter its honorary legal adviser. Together they identified on a large-scale map every small plot of land within a four-mile radius of the London Central Post Office which had not yet been built over. On closer inspection many of these small spaces turned out to be burial grounds. Members of the Kyrle Society wrote to the trustees responsible for their upkeep, suggesting how these grounds might be converted into public gardens by removing gravestones, planting flowerbeds, constructing pathways and installing seats. The response was not very encouraging. The gates of most of the graveyards, like those of the Garden of Love in William Blake's *Songs of Experience*, remained firmly locked. On her walks through the most densely built-up parts of the city, Octavia was disappointed to see how little open space there was which was not, in Blake's words, 'filled with graves and tombstones where flowers should be'.

There were, however, enough exceptions to convince her that it

Robert Hunter in the mid-1860s. The young lawyer began working for the Commons Preservation Society in 1868. (NT)

London going out of Town *or* The March of Bricks & Mortar. *George Cruikshank's caricature, published in 1829, attacking the devastation of rural Hampstead by jerry-builders. Housing built to accommodate the mass migration of workers into cities and towns was already presenting a perceived threat to open spaces and the countryside. (NT)*

John Ruskin, a self-portrait, 1874. (Ruskin Foundation, University of Lancaster)

The Hinksey road-menders, 1874. On the left is John Ruskin's gardener, David Downes, who helped Octavia Hill with her urban gardens. Third from left is Alfred, later Viscount Milner, and fourth is Hardie Rawnsley, then an undergraduate at Oxford. (Oxfordshire Photographic Archive Centre)

Hardwicke Rawnsley, a photograph taken in 1885 by Rupert Potter, father of Beatrix. Hardie had shot to public attention two years earlier when, as Vicar of Wray, he had vociferously protested against the proposed railway from Braithwaite to Buttermere, and was popularly known as 'Defender of the Lakes'. (By permission of Rosalind Rawnsley)

Octavia Hill, a drawing by Edward Clifford, 1877. Already well-known for her housing work, at this period Octavia began campaigning to promote the importance of open spaces in urban areas, such as garden squares in London. (NT)

(Opposite page, top) The fourteenth-century Clergy House at Alfriston in Sussex, from a photograph taken in 1894. The National Trust began extensive repairs in 1896, having bought the house from the Ecclesiastical Commissioners for £10. (NT)

(Opposite) The medieval courthouse at Long Crendon, Buckinghamshire, in 1895. The architect C.R. Ashbee urged National Trust ownership so that the building might be used as an arts and crafts centre for poor children from London. When the Trust took the courthouse in 1900, Ashbee was astonished to find his plan defeated by Octavia Hill. He resigning from the Trust's Council deploring the acquisition of 'a mere dead lumber house with no humanity in it but just to be looked at by tourists'. (NT)

OUR PLEA FOR OPEN SPACES.

Octavia Hill's 'fairy godmother' image made her a target for satirists. Here she is depicted as Spring by Linley Sambourne in Punch in June 1883 following one of many appeals for public subscriptions. (Punch)

189

National Trust Executive Meeting, 15 April 1912, a watercolour painted by 'TMR' twelve years later. Beneath a portrait of Shaw-Lefevre, founder of the Commons Preservation Society, sits the Chairman, Sir Robert Hunter, listening to the botanist, Francis Oliver, who stands to speak 'on the charm of Blakeney Point'. On Hunter's

right stands Canon Rawnsley, the Secretary. Octavia Hill was absent from the meet-
ing through serious illness, but is nonetheless painted in attendance on the extreme
right. (NT)

A regatta at Barmouth on the Merionethshire coast of Wales in 1909. Dinas Oleu, the National Trust's first property, consists of four and a half acres of hillside to the left of the house near the top of the cliff. It was given by Fanny Talbot in 1895 to prevent further building and to preserve for public enjoyment a magnificent view over Cardigan Bay. (NT)

Barrington Court, a sixteenth-century manorhouse in Somerset, from a photograph tak c. 1890 when it was used as a cider store. It was the first substantial country house to l taken by the National Trust, in 1907, but the restoration costs proved so great that no further acquisitions of stately homes were made for almost thirty years. (NT)

was worthwhile to continue the campaign. The Rector of St George's-in-the-East agreed to open the greater part of his large churchyard once he had compiled an inventory of the tombstones to be removed, and with financial aid from the Metropolitan Board of Works he was enabled to purchase an adjacent Wesleyan burial ground to add to the total space. This project attracted several benefactors, and within a short time Octavia could claim that it was a total success:

> the churchwarden gave the fountain, and the vestry, instead of having to be urged on to spend more, actually ordered 24,000 bulbs this spring to make the place bright and pretty! The high wall covered with spikes which separated the church from the dissenting burial ground, has been pulled down, and the whole thrown into one. The ground has been laid out with grass, flower beds, broad gravel walks, and plenty of seats have been placed there. The day I was last there, there were many people in the garden, one or two evidently convalescents. The ground was in perfect order, a gardener and one man being in attendance.

She went on to observe:

> the people though evidently of the lower class, were clearly impressed with a feeling that the garden should be respected. In fact the special feature of this garden seemed to me to be the evident sense of its being common property – something that everyone had had a share in doing, and in which they had a common interest.[23]

Common interest or not, the conversion had cost the Vestry £1,200 and the Board of Works £3,000, considered by some to be an extravagant use of public funds. However, a sizeable and popular public garden had been gained.

The churchyard of St John's in Waterloo Road was the next to be transformed, although this time a substantial proportion of the money required was raised by voluntary subscription in order to forestall any criticism. The cleric who co-operated with this scheme was described by Octavia as 'a man of culture who loves plants and colour'.

> The Rev. Arthur Robinson has collected £290, and is laying it out more like a country garden, and less like a place

planned by a Board of Works, than any other I have seen.
He has stumps prepared for ferns to grow on ... a nice
bank, winding walks between the turf, knows which side
of the church his wisteria will grow, spoke with hope of
getting the large blue clematis to flower, wants numberless
creepers to cover the church walls, and to wreathe around
and make beautiful the few tombs which he leaves unmoved
because relatives are still living and care to retain them.[24]

A plot of ground behind Samuel Barnett's church, when cleared,
made another useful public garden, and a small burial ground on
Drury Lane was put in order for a mere £160. This was no sooner
opened, however, than there were reports of vandalism. It seemed
at first that the Kyrle Society's worst fears had been realised. There
was a great body of opinion prepared to argue that the poorer
classes were not fit to be allowed in to open spaces, and bad publicity could easily put an end to the opening of any further small
public gardens. Octavia's friend and colleague, Emma Cons, was
immediately despatched to see what had happened. To everyone's
relief she was able to report that the damage was entirely accidental.

the people availed themselves in such crowds of the
privilege of going in, that the ivy was very much trampled
on, and the yuccas which had been planted in the middle
of the gravel without any sort of protection had their leaves
spoiled; but the shrubs were hardly injured, nor does there
appear to have been any intentional mischief done.[25]

This incident merely served to strengthen the Kyrle Society's
conviction that there was an urgent need to secure free public
access to many more open spaces in central London. With renewed
vigour Octavia turned her attention to the famous squares in the
heart of the city. These were locked private gardens accessible only
to the owners of adjacent properties. During the extended summer
holidays they were virtually empty and unused. Now was the
time, Octavia decided, for more of the squares to be made generally accessible. She launched an appeal – an appeal which was to be
issued annually for nearly 70 years without result. Its recommendations were finally accepted in relation to *some* of the squares, but
it might usefully be re-issued today. Her pleas with the School
Board to consider opening school playgrounds on summer
evenings, on Saturdays and during school holidays, likewise met
with opposition. Such a concession would necessarily entail the

employment of play supervisors: a burden on the rates.

The Metropolitan Board of Works and city companies however were not unsympathetic to Octavia's ideas and they were prepared to back both the Kyrle Society and the CPS in support of new legislation. In 1877 the first Metropolitan Open Spaces Act gave the Board power to acquire certain categories of land and convert it for leisure use, a measure followed and extended by a statute of 1881 which permitted landowners and trustees in London to enter into a variety of agreements with the Metropolitan or district authorities, to convey 'open space in trust for the enjoyment of the public'.[26] In 1884, one of the shortest and most effective of Conservation Acts ever passed brought protection to thousands of unbuilt acres in cities and throughout the countryside. It made illegal the erection of any building, except for the enlargement of a place of public worship, upon any disused burial ground.

One of the greatest achievements of the Kyrle Society in collaboration with the CPS was the saving of Burnham Beeches. In June 1879 a newspaper advertisement announced the sale by auction of the manor which included these fine woods. The sale particulars represented the common rights as being of little importance, clearly implying that the buyer should have no difficulty in enclosing the estate. 'At all events', declared Shaw-Lefevre, 'there was a danger that a wanton purchaser might do so, and might cut down the celebrated beeches, or otherwise interfere with the beauties of the place.'[27] Officers of the CPS recalled that it had been a previous threat to common rights at Burnham in the 1850s which had persuaded John Stuart Mill to change his mind about the economic benefits of wholesale enclosures. Those rights had since fallen into disuse and they feared that they would be difficult to enforce. The surest way of protecting the trees would be to arrange for the purchase of the ground on which they stood by a party sympathetic to their preservation and to the maintenance of public access.

The Beeches were just within the 25 mile range of the Metropolitan Open Spaces Act, and a deputation from the Kyrle Society and the CPS was thus able to make joint representation to a committee of the Corporation of London, requesting them to buy the land. On looking further into the proposal, however, it appeared that the Corporation's powers, whilst effective in relation to the 374 acres of the disputed Common, would not at this time allow the purchase of the additional 175 acres of freehold which formed part of the holding. Undeterred by this obstacle, Bob Hunter negotiated with the vendors for first refusal of the property at a fixed price for one week. He then turned for help to Henry Peek. Without even inspecting the property, Peek agreed to buy the estate in its entirety, subsequently dividing it and selling that part containing the woods to London Corporation for £6,000, 'not a tenth part of the value of the land', according to Shaw-Lefevre.[28]

The purchase and possession of open spaces by local authorities was increasingly becoming the policy of the CPS in addition to the protection of commoners' rights. Through the Kyrle Society, Octavia was taking the lead in this direction. In a letter dated 9 May 1879 she specifically requests that her Society's Open Space Committee take cognisance of 'the much larger work you propose to yourselves than the CPS does ... that you have to encourage gift and purchase and beautifying as well as "preservation"; that you have to do with *private* land as well as *commons*'.[29] The all-embracing concept which gave rise to this policy would in due course lead to the foundation of the National Trust.

Open spaces played the most important part in the Kyrle Society's first prospectus, but as its membership grew, the organisation extended its activities. The Open Spaces Committee arranged for the regular distribution of plants and flowers to the homes of the sick and poor. Another committee dealt with aspects of musical education and performance, recruiting a choir to sing in various churches, hospitals and workhouses. Social evenings and entertainments were organised for the community halls which were becoming an integral part of Octavia's housing schemes. Occasionally a theatre was hired for amateur stage productions and comic opera, with scenery designed by Arthur Rackham. Assisted by William Morris, a third branch of the Kyrle Society arranged for public halls and hospital wards to be decorated with frescoes and mottoes, and a fourth group organised a free public library.

Smoke abatement was another concern of the Society. The problem of air pollution had attracted the attention of Select committees and had been the subject of several Acts of Parliament, the most recent of which, in 1863, had ordered the setting up of the Inspectorate of Alkali Industries in 1863/4. Pressure groups such as the Noxious Vapours Association in Manchester were formed, with the object of persuading local authority nuisance committees to curb the emissions from mill chimneys. Ruskin had taken up the issue in his lecture *The Storm Cloud of the Nineteenth Century*, describing the appearance over Europe of a 'sulphurous chimney-pot vomit of blackguardly cloud' and a new kind of 'plague wind'.[30]

During the nineteenth century the production of coal had increased twenty-fold and in London the weekly death-rate rose by nearly 40 per cent following a period of that smog described by

Dickens in *Bleak House* as 'London Particular'. The Alkali Inspectorate recorded, in the vicinity of Widnes and St Helens, extensive
damage to crops and trees. The Report of 1867 gives the first scientific description of the effects of acid rain and vapour:

> There is a clear distinction between damage done by a storm
> and that by bad vapour. The latter *shrivels* and curls up the
> leaves, does not break them off or make them ragged. A
> storm never discolours the bark of a shrub tree, or makes
> it fast to the stem. Bad vapour does both ... In the park ...
> the trees showed damage on the E. and N.E. sides, and
> particularly two rows of large elms. These elms are getting
> worse every year; this year's shoots all burnt on the sides
> above-named ...
>   In an orchard and garden near the chimney-pot
> manufactory the damage was very great this season; almost
> every leaf and shoot burnt up ...
>   August 17th – Valuing damage to crops today in Weston,
> near Runcorn ... The damage done to the crops here since
> June 20th has been to a great amount, and the works at
> Weston are entirely chemical. The village of Halton this
> afternoon was full of vapour, which affected both eyes and
> breathing. This village is two miles from the works. All the
> crops between the village and the works were then receiving
> damage.[31]

The Public Health Act of 1875 stated that industry should 'as far
as possible consume the smoke arising from the combustible
therein' but did not touch on the question of pollution from domestic sources, or introduce any controls which would hamper manufacturing processes.[32] During a brief stop in Nuremberg in 1880 on
her way home from a holiday in Greece with Harriot Yorke,
Octavia could not help but compare that city with the manufacturing towns of her own country:

> Trees grow among the houses, and children play round
> them, and clean industrious women knit at their doors ...
> and still these gardens for the people look reproach at me,
> when I think of England; every tree and creeper and space
> of green grass in the town reminds me of our unconsumed
> smoke, and how it poisons our plants, and dims the colour
> of all things for us.[33]

Once back in London, she sought the help of manufacturers and scientists to mount a display of improved fuels and grates. This exhibition generated considerable interest. Nothing like it had ever been seen before. None the less, 80 years were to elapse before legislation would be introduced to enforce a substantial reduction in atmospheric pollution.

The Kyrle society attracted all kinds of new ideas and a coterie of wealthy supporters. Royalty, aristocracy and several leading figures in the art world were drawn into its activities. Its image was that of a fairy-godmother to the poorest classes. Its great recommendation, according to Octavia, was that it improved the life of the poor without undermining their independence, diverting charitable funds from doles, which 'pauperised' the recipients, to making beautiful the environment.[34] HRH Princess Louise, Duchess of Argyll, was appointed vice-president, and she and Octavia became close friends. Princess Louise, the sixth child of Queen Victoria and a gifted sculptress, assisted the organisation financially and practically. So did Sir Frederick Leighton, who attended the Kyrle Society meetings in his capacity as President of the Royal Academy. The Duke of Westminster was also drawn in as chairman. On 2 November 1884 the Society's Public Meeting was held in the Rubens Room of his London home, Grosvenor House, off Park Lane.[35] All three, in association with Octavia, were to be active in the early work of the National Trust.

Of the numerous voluntary organisations spawned of Victorian optimism, none more effectively embraced the Arcadian spirit. The Kyrle Society's stated aim was to bring 'beauty home to the people in the widest and most catholic sense'. It inevitably became a target for ridicule, especially in *Punch*. But even mocking approval was considered better than silence, and the Society's treasurer never missed an opportunity to appeal for funds for the cause now nearest her heart. She wrote to *The Times* on 9 July 1886:

> Sir,
>
> In a few days the Kyrle Society hope to open a garden in Deptford for the people. We want money to complete the garden, and to provide other such.
>
> Will those of your readers who are about to leave London for the snow-heights of Switzerland, the winding fjords of Norway, the green woodlands or breezy seashore of England, consider the thousands to whom such gardens will afford the only change of air that August will bring? Give the fountain, you who will have the sea; plant the

plane trees, place the seats, you to whom the woodlands
will soon be accessible; provide small clearances among the
houses, from which a somewhat larger space of sky is
visible than our courts and streets can afford, you who know
that soon below your feet will lie stretched the whole
expanse of sun-lighted plain and over whose head will bend
the great space of fair summer sky.

I am, Sir,

Yours truly,
Octavia Hill

CHAPTER 4

Hardwicke Rawnsley

From the point of view of assessing their intrusion on the land-scape, there are many parallels between the building of railways in the nineteenth century and the construction of motorways and trunk roads 100 years later. Some time elapsed before it was generally realised that as well as enormous improvements in mobility and efficiency, both these revolutionary transport developments brought in their wake unforeseen disadvantages. In each case, organised protest against damage to the environment was slow to gather momentum. In the late 1950s there was only a short delay in determining the final line of the first section of the M1, but ten years later, when the Council for the Preservation of Rural England and other conservation bodies had mobilised their forces, the route of the M4 was the subject of heated controversy.

Just one example of the damaging effect of railways on open spaces in the nineteenth century can be seen in the lines radiating from Clapham Junction. Built in the 1850s without any protest, they trisect Wandsworth Common. At Banstead Common, the ease with which the Inclosure Commissioners allowed the London and Brighton Railway to cut a line through the downs, suggested to the Lord of the Manor the feasibility of extensive enclosures.

By the late 1860s the CPS, realising the threat to common land posed by railway construction, was lobbying Members of Parliament, who successfully moved the rejection of a number of railway bills including those which would have authorised the intersection of Hampstead Heath and allowed further intrusions into Barnes and Mitcham Commons. When, in 1877, the railway companies tried a second time to invade these open spaces Shaw-Lefevre won acceptance of a rule that in future the promoters of all private bills be required to advertise the effects of their proposals on common land in local newspapers and the pages of the *London Gazette*. Commons were liable to be violated not only for the building of railways, but for sewage farms, cemeteries and reservoirs; indeed any scheme intended to benefit the community as a whole.

Areas of beautiful countryside, both commons and private land remote from towns and cities, were sometimes equally at risk; for an improvement which on first impact seemed easily assimilated in the midst of vast scenery might later be cited as justification for despoliation. In the early 1860s the Penrith to Cockermouth Railway was built without any opposition on the grounds that it could spoil the valleys of the northern Lake District. On 14 October 1973, however, nearly 1,000 people assembled on the slopes of Latrigg to protest, when a motorway feeder road was planned to follow almost the same route. The objectors to the scheme might have succeeded if the abandoned railway had not provided a path for the highway. The new A66, excessively large for the volume of its traffic, is now a disfiguring scar on the floor of the Keswick valley.[1]

Railways in the Lake District had been under construction since the 1840s. Principally they were intended as an aid to mineral extraction, already a defacement of the fells, but the lines also carried passengers: local people, day excursionists, wealthy industrialists with villas on the shores of Windermere. Wordsworth, whose *Guide to the Lakes* (1810) helped make the region famous for its scenery, was mocked as an opponent of progress, when, in 1844, he argued strongly against the Kendal and Windermere railway in letters to the *Morning Post*. Some 32 years later, in a preface to a pamphlet protesting against the proposed extension of this railway to Ambleside and Keswick, Ruskin sourly declared that its achievement for tourism would be to 'open taverns and skittle grounds around Grasmere, which will soon, then, be nothing but a pool of drainage, with a beach of broken ginger-beer bottles'.[2] In 1883, Hardie Rawnsley, the young and impetuous vicar of Wray-on-Windermere, at last made the menace posed by railways to Lake District solitude an issue of national importance. He prevented the building of a line to carry slate across the Vale of Newlands, and inadvertently found himself at the forefront of opposition to any scheme which threatened to spoil the region's unique landscape.

Hardwicke Drummond Rawnsley was born on 18 September 1851 in the old rectory at Shiplake-on-Thames, opposite the church where the poet Tennyson, a distant relation and close family friend, was married by his father, the Reverend Drummond Rawnsley, in the year before Hardwicke's birth. Hardie, the twin of Frances Anna, was one of ten children. His mother Catherine, whose parents had died in India, had been brought up as the ward of her uncle, the arctic explorer Sir John Franklin, to whom there is a memorial in Westminster Abbey, and a statue in Waterloo Place, above the Mall.

The rectory garden, with its terraces sloping down towards the river, commands a magnificent view of the countryside to the south. In the foreground the 'eyots' with their tall poplars part the slow waters, providing a haven for the swans and shelter for the abundant wildlife. Lush pastures beyond the river stretch as far as the eye can see. Hardie spent the early years of his childhood in this idyllic setting, fishing, shooting rabbits and trapping birds with his elder brother Willingham; and with his sisters he studied the wild flowers. Botany was to be a lifelong enthusiasm.

The winter meadows, flooded and frozen, were ideal for sliding, and in summer the children joined in the haymaking. Their companions were the river folk; lock-keepers and mill men, setting willow traps for the fresh water eels. At Christmas, undeterred by heights, Hardie would climb the ladder to the top of the church tower, where he cut and cast down trails of ivy to his sisters, for the decoration of the sanctuary. He was never to forget those happy years. 'The sound of the bells borne down the stream, the chalk cliff and the violets, all these, though I left Shiplake when I was ten years old, had made impressions on me for life.'[3]

On the death of Hardie's grandfather, Thomas Rawnsley, in 1861, Drummond took over his father's parish at Halton Holgate, a village already familiar to the children as a stop on the journey to Skegness, where they spent holidays in a cottage shared with the Tennysons.

Skegness, on the edge of the Lincolnshire marshes, was then a very small resort, a place of pure delight for the children. 'We abandoned boots and socks the first hour we arrived', recalled Hardie, 'and never put them on again except to walk to church on Sunday.'[4] They could run out of the first floor of the cottage straight onto the Roman sea wall by means of a plank, and for the rest of the day be lost in the dunes. They would pester the old coastguards and shrimpers; sailors who had fought alongside Nelson and delighted to tell them tales of voyages and sea battles. Hardie's memory of that coastal landscape remained vivid all his life: 'mud that shone like burnished ore. Nothing but the great stakes that guided the fisherboats at flow of tide ... the cry of stints or curlew ... sea-wilderness, devoid of man.'[5]

Eleven miles inland the countryside below Halton Holgate, the flat expanse of the fens with 'drains' and windmills, now became Hardie's territory. His new home on the edge of the Lincolnshire wold overlooked an old drovers' road cut deep into the greensand rock. An elegant foot bridge once spanned the cutting, linking the rectory to the parish church; Hardie remembered watching the village carpenter at work on its construction.[6] A few years after the move to Halton, he witnessed the building of the Firsby to Spilsby railway with its intermediate station for the village. It was a development which, despite its many benefits, was to impinge on the peace and tranquillity of the surrounding countryside and erode the self-sufficiency and independence of the community.

At the age of eleven Hardie was sent to Uppingham, whose headmaster, Edward Thring, was one of the foremost educators of the nineteenth century. It was unusual by comparison with other public schools; the boys enjoyed respect and privacy and in addition to academic subjects were taught drawing, carpentry, music and even athletics. Thring had set up the first ever school gymnasium in England and had employed a professionally trained German gymnast, Carl Beseigel, to run it.[7]

Due to his father's high expectations Hardie made a difficult start, but once a scholarship had been achieved he felt more at ease and entered wholeheartedly into the school's many activities. He excelled at athletics and gymnastics, wrote copiously for the school magazine and developed a remarkable skill in taxidermy. The stuffing of birds and 'small deer' was carried on in his study which in hot weather 'was an object of marked interest ... but at a safe distance'.[8]

At Uppingham, Hardie was encouraged to develop his literary interests and his latent talent for verse writing. During his time in the sixth form, Thring invited him to join his family on holiday in the Lake District, to climb the fells and visit the places associated with the Lake poets. This instruction had a profound effect. Ever after Hardie felt compelled to pen a sonnet on every conceivable occasion.

Assessing the boy's academic work, Thring observed serious lapses of concentration: 'I used to blow him up for overworking and for indolence, and for want of steadiness of purpose – we have had many an onset.'[9]

In 1870 Hardie went up to Balliol College, Oxford, where Dr Jowett, the famous Greek scholar, had recently been appointed

Master. The College already had a high reputation and Jowett spared neither himself nor his pupils in his determination to achieve the highest academic standards. He once described his mission as making his students 'properly ambitious'. Hardie was likeable, well-mannered and as an Uppingham boy should be, extremely fit. He was not the Master's ideal undergraduate, however, spending more time happily engaged in ballad-singing, ragging and other sociable activities than in study. Jowett advised him against writing verses and would have been disturbed to know that Hardie had demonstrated his prowess at high jump in a crowded street by leaping over a donkey cart, complete with passenger: 'You must get rid of all excitable ways which will altogether unfit you for any place of responsibility or authority.'[10] One of his tutors, the philosopher Thomas Hill Green, was more sympathetic. He discerned a young man not academically brilliant, like his fellow-Uppinghamian and tutor Richard Lewis Nettleship, but one who was undoubtedly dynamic and practical.

John Ruskin, by this time Slade Professor of Art in Oxford, was awakening the social conscience of many undergraduates. Hardie met him at a College breakfast, exhorting those at table to join the Hinksey road-menders, repairing a muddy lane linking the city with a village whose inhabitants were mainly poor labourers. At various times the roll-call of famous intellectual navvies included Arnold Toynbee, Oscar Wilde and Alfred (later Viscount) Milner; supervised by Ruskin's long-suffering gardener, David Downes.

For Hardie, the Hinksey labour was a welcome diversion. He had given up classics in favour of Natural Science, and in 1874 gained a respectable Third. By that time, he had decided to follow his father and grandfather into the Church. As a first step, early the next year he began work as an assistant in a hostel for down-and-outs, administered by the rector of St Mary's in Soho. With a recommendation from Ruskin, he made himself known to Octavia Hill, then at the height of her career as a housing reformer. He was eager to join in the work, and willingly accepted charge of a rent round under the guidance of Emma Cons.[11]

He drove himself too hard, and within a few months suffered a severe nervous breakdown. Octavia at once arranged a period of convalescence at Croft, on the northern shore of Lake Windermere. There Hardie was looked after by her friends, the Fletchers, who had three daughters, Alice, Edith and Helen, who shared many of his interests. They spent the days together, boating, and walking on Loughrigg Fell. Occasionally, Hardie would visit Thring at Grasmere, and his cousin at Wray Castle.

By the Autumn, he was fully recovered. With a reference from Thring, Hardie succeeded in obtaining a post in a working-class suburb of Bristol. He was ordained deacon, and given the responsibility of setting up a mission to the poor, funded by Clifton College public school, then under the headmastership of the Reverend Dr John Percival, later Bishop of Hereford.

Hardie first found a large room on the upper floor of a building which had once been a carpenter's workshop, and converted it into a small church. The congregation at his services included a number of unruly youths, whom he referred to as his 'lambs'. It was not uncommon for prayers to be punctuated by the rattle of stones hurled by their friends in the street below, or for a fracas to break out inside the building. When violence erupted, Hardie would suspend the divine office and leap into the fray in the capacity, as he put it, of 'half parson, half policeman'.[12]

Living conditions in the parish were the worst he had ever seen. Rows of jerry-built houses had been erected on land which was periodically flooded by the River Frome. Some of his parishioners were squatters living in sheds, tolerated by the municipal authorities on condition that they did not try to erect more permanent dwellings. Hardie's role was that of a 'domestic missioner' establishing a variety of activities centred around a Temperance Club. At weekends he organised a football team and took the boys on Sunday afternoon walks in the countryside.

It was during his two years at the mission that Hardie was involved in a campaign to save the tower of St Werburgh, part of a disused fourteenth-century church about to be demolished. After many representations to the city authorities, to ensure its preservation the tower was taken down stone-by-stone, and re-erected on another site.[13]

The self-confidence which Hardie regained in Bristol was to be his undoing. The Temperance Club, though successful, was at times riotous, and consistently lost money. His 'lambs' were high-spirited and noisy, making cat-calls at passers-by on their country outings. When disciplined by Dr Percival, Hardie was unrepentant, and refused to change his ways. He was promptly dismissed. A petition signed by 300 of his parishioners failed to achieve his reinstatement. Percival branded the petitioners 'hard-and-fast dissenters', and went on to savage Hardie's character in a letter to Thring, who immediately sprang to his defence, but to no avail.[14] Had it not been for Thring's continued support and the intervention of his relatives, Hardie's career in the Church might have ended here.

The little church of St Margaret at Wray-on-Windermere was in the gift of Hardie's cousin. A Lake District parish with 100 souls and a stipend of £100 per annum it was a far cry from the city mission, but a chance not to be missed. He passed the diocesan examinations and was ordained priest in Carlisle Cathedral on 23 December 1877, barely three months after his dismissal from Bristol. A month later he married Edith Fletcher in Brathay Church, near Croft. He had proposed to her that autumn during a holiday in the West Country. His father came up to conduct the ceremony with the assistance of Edward Thring and Lewis Nettleship, on a cold bright winter's day which made the snowclad fells seem like bridesmaids to the occasion. Following the wedding, Hardie and Edith set out for their new home – the ivy-covered vicarage of Low Wray, two miles to the south, on the edge of a gentle valley sloping down to the western shore of the lake. Wray reminded Hardie of his childhood.

The winter of 1877/8 was one of the coldest on record. Windermere was frozen so hard that it was possible to skate from High Wray as far as Belle Island, a distance of two and a half miles. At weekends, excursionists from the industrial towns of Lancashire packed the local trains from Oxenholme; they joined day trippers from Kendal jostling one another to be first on the ice. The hotels at Bowness served take-away hot-pots, a picnic which if inadvertently left on the ice, as Hardie observed, would burn a hole, down which it would disappear. On the freezing air, sounds from the Lake in the early evening darkness recalled to him lines from Wordsworth's *The Prelude*:

> ... All shod with steel
> We hissed along the polished ice in games
> Confederate, imitative of the chase
> And woodland pleasures, – the resounding horn
> The pack loud chiming, and the hunted hare.
> So through the darkness and the cold we flew,
> And not a voice was idle; with the din
> Smitten, the precipices rang aloud;
> The leafless trees and every icy crag
> Tinkled like iron; while far distant hills
> Into the tumult sent an alien sound
> Of melancholy not unnoticed, while the stars
> Eastward were sparkling clear, and in the west
> The orange sky of evening died away.[15]

The incessant activity on the eastern shore of Windermere merely served to accentuate the quiet solitude of Wray. Even at the height of summer, visitors were seldom seen in the parish in great numbers. The last quarter of the nineteenth century saw the beginning of a long depression in agriculture and the gradual depopulation of rural villages. Imports of cheap grain from North America were hastening the widespread conversion of farmland from arable to pasture, displacing farm labour. Although the Lake counties were not as vulnerable in this respect as lowland areas, they were none the less seriously affected. Hardie and Edith started wood-carving classes in the winter evenings, to help relieve the unemployment.

Wray was a welcome contrast to the frenzy and frustrations of Bristol, but its tranquillity was not something Hardie enjoyed for too long. By the beginning of his second year in the parish he and Edith, both young and energetic, decided they needed a break from the slow, gentle rhythms of village life. They took advantage of a last-minute invitation to join a small party planning a six-month trip to the Near East and the Holy Land. Hardie hastily procured a locum and sent a note – not a request, but a note – to an astonished Bishop Goodwin, telling him of his intentions. He and Edith then set off, picking up passports from a London Post Office on the afternoon of their departure. Two months on camel-back visiting the Pyramids, then on to Petra, Gaza, Beersheba, Hebron and Jerusalem. Hardie lingered in Jerusalem to indulge his enthusiasm for amateur archaeology at Micmash. From Jerusalem they continued by way of the snowcapped Lebanon ridge to Damascus and Beirut, collecting cones from the famous cedars, and returning home by way of Cyprus, Constantinople and Greece.

Travel was to become an insatiable passion. Nearly every year they spent a few weeks in the Alps. One of the fruits of their many visits was a delightful book called *Flower-time in the Oberland* (1904), written by Hardie and illustrated with sketches by Edith. After their first Grand Tour, Hardie regularly visited more distant destinations. In 1896 he was sent as a reporter to Russia to witness the coronation of the Czar and three years later spent several weeks in America as roving ambassador for the National Trust, selling its aims and ideals to prospective supporters in New England. He returned to Egypt on several occasions, and was an active participant in several archaeological excavations. After every trip, he returned full of enthusiasm for what he had seen and done. Many evenings were subsequently taken up in lecturing to local societies, who in the days before radio and television were always in need of an entertaining speaker.

Two years after his first trip to Egypt and the Holy Land, Hardie published his *Sonnets at the English Lakes* (1881) (erroneously recorded by *The Times* in his obituary as 'Sunset at the English Lakes'). Of all the poems in this slim and beautifully bound volume, *The Squirrel* is perhaps the most delightful:

Light-hearted dweller in the voiceless wood
Pricking thy tasselled ears in hope to tell
Where, under, in thy haste, the acorn fell:
Now, for excess of summer in thy blood,
Running through all thy tricksy change of mood,
Or vaulting upward to thy citadel
To seek the mossy nest, the miser-cell,
And chuckle o'er thy winter's hoard of food.
Miser? I do thee wrong to call thee so,
For, from the swinging larch-plumes overhead,
In showers of whispering music thou dost shed
Gold, thick as dust, where'er thy light feet go;
Keep, busy Almoner, thy gifts of gold!
Be still! Mine eyes ask only to behold.[16]

The summer of 1882 was the first occasion on which Hardie met Beatrix Potter, when her family were staying at Wray Castle, a large mock-baronial house overlooking the lake. Her father, Rupert Potter, was a gifted photographer; an interest he shared with the Rawnsleys. Beatrix was an extremely shy 16-year-old who had been left very much alone, and had consequently withdrawn into her own interior existence. She and her brother Bertram had created a fantasy world which Hardie readily understood. They collected plants and insects, skinned and preserved dead animals and kept live ones, which they had smuggled into the schoolroom, as pets. They sketched and painted pictures of their captives in human dress going about human business, and Beatrix later invented stories about them. Had it not been for Hardie's encouragement, such tales as *Peter Rabbit*, *The Tailor of Gloucestor*, *Jemima Puddleduck*, *Mrs Tiggy-Winkle* and *Squirrel Nutkin* might never have been written for publication.

Beatrix Potter's success as an author and illustrator of nursery stories gave her the confidence to build a life of her own as an active Lake District farmer and sheep-breeder. She later bought farmland and cottages with the National Trust specifically in mind, and on her death bequeathed to the organisation over 4,000

acres of land.[17] During long summer holidays in the years following her first acquaintance with the Rawnsleys, she became a
frequent companion of their only son Noël, who was some years
younger than herself. In later life Noël maintained that Beatrix was
the real love of his father's life.

A few months after his first meeting with Beatrix, Hardie was
drawn into an issue which would effectively place him in the lime-
light and in a role he would energetically fill for the rest of his life.
Robert Somervell, manager of a successful shoe factory in Kendal,
had become a close friend during Hardie's period of convalescence
at Croft. As a keen local historian and an admirer of the Lake
District's unique and unspoilt scenery, Somervell was concerned
about the future development of the region. His active involvement in conservation began in 1875 when, in response to the high
demand for pig-iron following the Franco-Prussian War, the Grasmere side of Helvellyn was scarred by workings for deposits of
iron ore. Greater mining activity in the Lake District would
increase pressure to permit the building of railways, both to
service the mines and to facilitate access to the whole area. Seeing
what a serious threat to the environment this would pose,
Somervell organised a petition to Parliament. He sent his ware-
houseman, Joe Littlewood, canvassing signatures at every hotel
and household along the route of a projected line from Windermere, the existing railhead, to join the Cockermouth to Penrith line
at Keswick. Such a line would cut the natural barrier formed by
Dunmail Raise, at the heart of the Lake District, effectively destroying this mountain fastness.

Fortunately the petition turned out to be unnecessary. The
increased demand for iron ore did not last long, and a railway
without mining traffic would not be an economic proposition.

The next threat to the Lake District appeared without warning.
Manchester Corporation put forward an outrageous scheme to
dam and turn into a huge reservoir the remote and beautiful
Thirlmere, then a long and narrow stretch of shallow water, edged
with reeds and marshes, a haven for waders and wildfowl. A
protest meeting was hastily summoned at the Prince of Wales
Hotel in Grasmere, and a Thirlmere Defence Association was
formed. Somervell, although the youngest present, offered to write
a pamphlet setting out the objections. In addition he agreed to
circulate a petition from the campaign headquarters, set up in the
library of his home on the eastern shore of Windermere. He trav-

elled the country addressing meetings, including a gathering in Octavia Hill's home in London.

Everything seemed to be going extremely well. The press had in the main come out against the Corporation when, in 1878, the Bill for Thirlmere went before a Select Committee of Parliament. Suddenly, the protest went badly awry. Somervell and Octavia invited Bob Hunter to meet the Defence Association's steering committee, intending that he should be appointed to present the case to the Select Committee, making the aesthetic and recreational arguments the central issue. When they realised what was afoot the leading members of the Association were forced to show their true colours. It was not conservation they wanted, but compensation, the level of which they hoped would be increased by the publicity that Octavia Hill and Somervell were capable of generating. They feared that Bob Hunter might actually win the case, which was the last thing they wished for. The Association's spokesman made it clear, in no uncertain terms, that the committee had no intention of listening to Bob Hunter's suggestions. The open space movement's best legal adviser thereupon walked out of the meeting.[18]

From then on the fate of Thirlmere was sealed. Opposition to the parliamentary Bill went off at half-cock. The Select Committee found in favour of Manchester and the landowners of the Wythburn valley rejoiced. Large sums in compensation changed hands. Henceforward, as a break from his normal week's work in Kendal, and endless pleas to the Corporation to minimise the damage caused by their engineering works, for some welcome relaxation Somervell would row across Windermere to visit the Rawnsleys. Sad to say, even Hardie was not on his side. Having spent two years in a parish that lacked basic amenities, he knew that if there was not to be a continuing danger of cholera, cities must have a safe and plentiful supply of fresh water; none the less, he approved wholeheartedly of Somervell's earlier protest against the threat of railways. Hardie would in due course accept an invitation to offer prayers at the ceremony which marked the completion of the Thirlmere pipeline. For the present it was Bishop Goodwin who wrote a letter to *The Times* expressing bitter sarcasm: 'that a time might come when instead of a trip to the Lakes we should hear of a trip to the tanks or a month at the reservoirs'.[19] Old prints are now the only reminder of Thirlmere as it was.

In August 1882, Hardie received news of the death of his father. The living of Halton Holgate was his for the asking, but by now the Lake District was so much a part of him that he could not imagine moving elsewhere. He would remain at Wray; a decision which was to have far-reaching consequences.

In the New Year a syndicate of nine quarry owners was discovered to be at an advanced stage of planning a single-track railway from Braithwaite, near Keswick, into the green slate deposits in cliffs above Buttermere. Somervell by this time had moved away to Cambridge, and the Bill approving the scheme had reached its parliamentary Committee stage before Hardie read about it in the press. The owner of an affected property had already taken up the cudgels, and Hardie wasted no time in adding his voice to the protest. Early in February the following letter appeared in *The Standard*:

Sir,

The public has not been warned a moment too soon, and owes a debt of gratitude to Mr. Greenall, Lingholme, Keswick, for having sounded the alarm. The question that the Select Committee of the House of Commons will have to decide is one of great interest, not only to us who are dwellers at the Lakes, but to all the thousands who crowd hither annually from stifling city and railway-haunted district to find peace and freedom from the bustle of their time. And the question simply stated is this – Are the proprietors who work a certain slate quarry up in Honister to be allowed to damage irretrievably the health, rest and pleasure ground of the whole of their fellow countrymen who come there for needed quiet and rest, in order that they – the owners – may put a few more shillings a truckload into their private pockets? And this when it can be proved that all the slate required can be carted to the train, and that the public are either willing to pay the price for carting that particular slate or can get as good elsewhere. Let the slate train once roar along the western side of Derwentwater, let it once cross the lovely vale of Newlands, and Keswick as the resort of weary men in search of rest will cease to be.

Each year these public grounds of recreation and health are narrowed and invaded by private greed, miscalled enterprise. When will true public spirit awake, and in the best interests of its age, and the generations of busy England yet unborn, protest and claim State protection in a matter that concerns the State only?

Your obedient servant,
H. D. Rawnsley[20]

Further letters to the press were written with the aid of W. H. Hills of Ambleside and Gordon Somervell, Robert's brother. Appeals were sent to friends and potential sympathisers. With encouragement from Bob Hunter and James Bryce, then Chairman of the CPS, a 'Borrowdale and Derwentwater Defence Fund' was set up. The CPS at the time was pursuing its campaign against proposed railways in Epping Forest, and this served to heighten public awareness of the menace of railways elsewhere in unspoilt scenery. With the backing of the CPS the protest in the Lake District was declared to be 'of national importance ... all classes resort to this locality for health, rest and recreation, its preservation is the concern of all'. From *The Times* and *The Spectator* downwards came a howl of consternation against the quarry owners. *Punch* rattled off a sarcastic poem:

What, ho, my merry Philistines here's news and no mistake,
They're going to run a railway round and spoil each pretty
      lake,
And near the famous cataract that Southey sang of yore
The locomotive's noise shall drown the murmur of Lodore.[21]

In Keswick opposition spilled onto the normally conservative pages of the *Westmorland Gazette*. Indifferent hoteliers were jolted out of their complacency as guide-book writer M. J. B. Baddeley pointed out to them the effect on their stage-coach traffic if the line was to carry passengers. Soon petitions were circulating throughout the British Isles. Campbell Fraser, one of many university professors who raised their voices in opposition to the quarry owners, having paid homage to the Lake poets, described the Lake region of Cumberland and Westmorland as 'Nature's own English University in the age of great cities'; it should 'bar the entrance of the Stygian locomotive'. To which the philosopher Edward Caird added his own voice, declaring that 'Parliament might as well sanction the taking of the canvases from their frames in the National Gallery to be used for towels, as give powers to the Braithwaite and Buttermere Railway.'[22] Ruskin added his name to the protest, but without much optimism. He saw the Lake Country as being in the same plight as Venice. Doomed by their own beauty, they must suffer the same fate.

Dear Rawnsley,
      You may always put my name without asking leave to
any petition against the railways anywhere. But it's all of

no use. You will soon have a Cook's tourist railway up
Scawfell and another up Helvellyn and another up
Skiddaw, and then a connecting line all round.

Yours affectionately,

J. Ruskin[23]

He was wrong. Within eight weeks the volume of protest had
reached such a pitch that the proprietors withdrew their Bill. The
tranquillity of the Newlands Valley was spared.

This was only the beginning. Three months later a second Bill, to
build a railway along the shores of Lake Ennerdale, was promulgated. *The Pall Mall Gazette* parodied Wordsworth:

> Wake England, wake! 'tis now the hour
> 	To sweep away this black disgrace –
> The want of locomotive power
> 	In so enjoyable a place.
> Nature has done her part, and why
> 	Is mightier man in his to fail?
> I want to hear the porter's cry,
> 	'Change here for Ennerdale'![24]

An indignant Hardie went up to London to give evidence before
the Select Committee in a blaze of publicity. The Ennerdale Railway Bill was thrown out. Quarry syndicates and railway barons re-
examined their plans. The proposed Great North Western line to
Ambleside was never to gain support and the London & North
Western branch line to the head of Ullswater was cancelled. The
tide of indiscriminate railway-building had begun to turn.
Wordsworth was vindicated at last.

Overnight the Vicar of Wray had become 'Defender of the
Lakes'. 'The victory is wholly due to your enthusiasm and energy',
wrote a delighted supporter. 'None of us would have done
anything but for you.'[25] At the annual meeting of the Wordsworth
Society in College Hall, Westminster, presided over by Matthew
Arnold, Hardie announced the formation of 'A Permanent Lake
District Defence Society'. He appealed for a guarantee fund of
£5,000.

Writing the constitution of the new organisation once all the fuss
had died down caused serious problems. From the outset, Hardie
wanted the Lake District Defence Society to include in its aims and
objects the protection of rights of way and access over commons.
His margin notes on the draft appeal leaflet advocated 'opposing

all enclosures of common land in the Lake District' and 'what about footpaths!!!' The LDDS should 'work in co-operation with the CPS and Kyrle Society'.[26] In the end these ideas came to nothing. Even the most determined local enthusiasts for the LDDS were ambivalent in their attitudes. Happy for arguments about rights of access to be used to support the protection of 'picturesque beauty', they did not want them to become the stated aims of the Society. They were nervous of being invaded by hordes of fell-walkers. They wanted both the penny and the bun.

Hardie had all along expressed his support of increased access to the region in evidence to the Select Committee in the Ennerdale Railway case. He gleefully quoted their response to the press: 'We are careful for the masses in refusing to allow their recreation ground to be made impossible for them in the future. Parliament does not forget that the work of the world demands that there shall be rest places for weary workers.'[27]

Despite the great play made of a shilling donation 'from a Birmingham working woman, in grateful remembrance of a holiday in the district', the LDDS had little prospect of representing the interests of 'weary workers'. An analysis of its membership of nearly 600 in the 1880s shows that those drawn from the intellectual, professional and managerial classes predominate: professors, clergy, public school masters, numerous Manchester merchants and Leeds industrialists. Fewer than 10 per cent were Lake District residents. More than a quarter of the membership lived in London and the Home Counties; a further quarter in Lancashire, mainly in Manchester. The remainder included a dozen Americans, most of them from colleges on the East Coast. Hardie excused the dearth of local representation with the patronising assertion 'that the inhabitants of the dales, who have their world of beauty "too much with them late and soon" are not the safest guardians of their lovely homes', a remark which elicited a swift response from his opponents. *The Whitehaven News* described the vicar and his allies as 'cheap aesthetes', 'noisy sentimentalists'. 'Cumberland people ... could look after their own interests without interference from outsiders who put the protection of scenery before the livelihoods of the locals.'[28]

Even though the LDDS was not as representative of all classes as Hardie would have liked, the paper had not grasped the essential point. Hardie could see that eventually

a wise Government may enable the Lake District to have a special Act to protect it from railroad outrage for the people, as has been done in Yellow-Stone Park, and partially in the Yosemite Valley of America (though there the State not only provided an Act, but first bought it up for the people's use).[29]

In 1810 Wordsworth had suggested that the Lake District should be 'a sort of national property, in which every man has a right and interest who has an eye to perceive and a heart to enjoy'.[30] Until that time no one since the Norman Conquest and the creation of Royal Forests had conceived that a large and integral area of unspoilt landscape ought to be legally protected. However, in spite of Hardie and the LDDS, it was not until 1951, 140 years after Wordsworth had first promulgated the idea, that the region was designated a national park.

In 1883 Bishop Goodwin invited Hardie to become Vicar of Crosthwaite, the parish church of Keswick. He was delighted to accept the appointment, and on 9 July, as rain clouds scudded over Castlerigg Fells, celebrated his installation by ringing the church bell 105 times. The tradition was that a new incumbent tolled the bell once for each of the years he intended to remain in the parish. Hardie was obviously intent on a long ministry! He and Edith moved into Crosthwaite Vicarage, which was once described by the poet Thomas Gray as 'the sweetest scene I can yet discover in point of pastoral beauty'. From the study window was a view which had been the envy of Robert Southey:

Mountains, lake and vale; the valley in glorious verdure,
Derwent motionless, grey, retaining every reflection . . .[31]

The parish church was founded in the sixth century, and there was much to appeal to Hardie's sense of history. He set about reviving the legend of its patron saint, Kentigern, whose symbols, a tree, a robin, a bell and a salmon with a ring in its mouth, he incorporated into the new mosaic pavement in the chancel. Several features of the church today, including the pavement, the reredos and the churchyard gates, were designed by Edith Rawnsley, who was largely responsible for the early work of the Keswick School of Industrial Arts (KSIA).

The KSIA was a venture begun by Edith and Hardie as a course of evening classes during the first winter, as at Wray, to try to counter unemployment caused by the agricultural depression and the seasonal nature of the tourist trade. The school soon grew to be a centre of excellence, particularly in the design and manufacture of domestic art metalwork in silver, brass and copper. The students, wrote Hardie

> use their eyes and see beauty in living design and the worth
> of a springing curve ... you will watch the men with
> pencil in hand doing what they may to reproduce a branch
> of wild rose upon their drawing boards, or modelling a
> cast of a leaf in clay ... [they] see what they used to pass
> by without notice in flower life and bird life, and beauty
> of light and shade, of cloud and sunshine, upon the fellside
> of their native vale.[32]

An offshoot of the school was the Ruskin Linen Industry, set up with the help of the Guild of St George, under the direction of Marion Twelves. She was responsible for the revival in the Lake District of hand-spinning, weaving, dyeing, embroidery and Greek lace-work. Miss Twelves and Edith Rawnsley were to organise the funeral palls which draped the coffins of both Tennyson and John Ruskin: hand-spun and woven unbleached linen, with an embroidered design consisting of trails of wild roses in a simple and restrained pattern, a laurel wreath and a quotation from their works.

The Keswick School of Industrial Arts endured for 100 years, and its earliest products are some of the finest inspired by the Arts and Crafts Movement. Soon after his arrival at Crosthwaite, Hardie invited Bishop Goodwin to plant in the churchyard a sapling grown from one of the cedar cones collected on his trip to the Holy Land. Prophetically perhaps, the mighty cedar of Lebanon which it became fell in a January gale in 1984. Later that year the KSIA closed its doors for the last time.

Keswick at the time of Hardie's ministry was primarily a market town, with some light industry in the form of pencil manufacture. Tourism in the area was well established, and had been extended in the 1870s to cater for working-class holidaymakers accommodated in the lodging houses and temperance hotels which had sprung up in the wake of the railway. Hardie frequently acted as guide for the Co-operative Holiday Fellowship, leading walks enlivened by his inimitable commentary on local and natural history.

With curates attending to the day-to-day running of his parish, Hardie soon established himself as a prominent figure on the Lakeland scene. He became the natural choice to chair meetings, deliver lectures and open fêtes, and was looked to as an authority on all customs and traditions of the Lake District. His presence was soon assumed at every conceivable gathering from sheep-dog trials at Troutbeck, the Mardale Shepherds Meet, sheep-shearing at West Head and Brig End, to Daffodil Day at Cockermouth, Rush Bearing at Ambleside and Grasmere and the pilgrimage to St Herbert's Island on Derwent Water. At the Grasmere Sports he would sit on a folding stool beneath an enormous black umbrella, protection against the expected driving rain, a flask of hot tea at his feet, a panting wrestler in breeches and flannel shirt by his side, surrounded by cloth-capped dalesmen:[33] He appeared to all the world to be the *genius loci*.

In spite of the fact that he was often intolerably authoritarian, described by the church gardener as 'a peppery old swine' and by another of his parishioners as 'the most active volcano in Europe', Hardie was quite capable of enjoying the humour of a tale against himself. He would often recount how in the course of his visiting, soon after his arrival in Crosthwaite, wearing a dark straw hat and open-necked shirt and bearing fruit from the vicarage orchard, an elderly and infirm parishioner mistook him for the church gardener. She kept him on the threshold, and instructed him to convey her thanks to the vicar.

He was involved in all aspects of local education, and was instrumental in the foundation of the Newton Rigg County Farm School. As the founder of Keswick High School, Hardie pioneered the idea of co-education, and did all he could to support the development of secondary education in the area. The Director of Education in Cumberland noted how Hardie 'in planning schemes of work for schools and schoolchildren ... would try and get in by hook or crook something in the way of music, singing or dancing as a humanising factor'.[34] His school songs and moral rhymes lived on in the memories of Lake District children for many years.

The May Queen ceremony in Keswick, established by Hardie in 1885, was a means of teaching children a respect for nature. The Queen's Proclamation, which he wrote, was handed to every child present. The first country code, it implored the children not to rob birds' nests, not to 'kill or hurt any living creature needlessly ... not to root up ferns, nor break down the blossoming trees, but shall learn the names of the flowers and their reasons and habits ...' 'I expect', declared Hardie, 'there will be fewer squirrels hunted in the Keswick woods and more care taken of the ferns and flowers in the Keswick lanes, by reason of her Gracious Majesty's command.'[35] He preached vigorously against vivisection, cruel trapping, rabbit-coursing and the shooting of owls, kestrels, buzzards and other birds for hat feathers. He joined the Manchester Fur and Feather Club, which later became the Royal Society for the Protection of Birds, sat on its first Council and accepted the honour of a vice-presidency, awarding the Cumbrian Schools Challenge Shield for 'Bird and Tree Day'.[36] Yet he also wrote in one of his books an account of an otter hunt which quite glossed over the issue of its barbaric cruelty.[37] Fortunately, not many schoolchildren would have read his books.

During the first few years of his ministry at Crosthwaite, Hardie was occupied almost entirely with matters of local importance. One issue, however, did not fail to attract controversy on a similar scale to the railway protests. Many myths and legends surround the Keswick footpaths dispute, and a true account is long overdue.

In 1884, James Bryce, a keen mountaineer who was at that time chairman of the CPS, introduced into Parliament an Access to Mountains Bill. It failed to command enough support to become law, and at this stage would have applied only to Scotland, where there was a strong Rights of Way Society. Nevertheless, its introduction increased public awareness of the fact that enclosures had substantially diminished the possibilities of walking and climbing in the most scenic parts of Britain. In the same year, the National Footpaths Preservation Society was founded by the writer Henry Allnut. The subscription was 5/– per annum or 10/6d including free legal advice. Within a year the NFPS, with 178 members and five affiliated groups, had been notified of 124 cases of footpath interference.

The rejection of Bryce's Bill, the first of a score of similar measures to be thrown out by Parliament, left unresolved an unfortunate state of affairs. Ramblers who felt they were being unfairly obstructed and wished to do something about it were faced with no alternative but to seek permission for access from every landowner whose estate they crossed, or else somehow to force a way through whatever hindrances were placed in their path. Wordsworth himself, in the company of the Lord Chief Justice and Justice Coleridge, had with bare hands torn down a wall blocking an old track between Ullswater and Lowther Castle. The Keswick and District Footpath Preservation Association, founded a few years after the poet's death, tried to keep alive his enthusiasm for maintaining mountain paths long before the formation of the NFPS, but it did not win much local support. To the south, on the other side of Dunmail Raise, in the vicinity of Ambleside, at least one footpath was closed every year.

In the Spring of 1885 two landowners near Keswick decided to prevent the public from walking tracks which had long been in use on their estates, and which were increasingly frequented by tourists. At another time they might have been successful. The introduction and rejection of Bryce's Bill, however, had infuriated ramblers, who were now looking for a test case to prove their rights of way.

One of these tracks gave access to the western shore of Derwent Water, the other to Latrigg fell in the lee of Skiddaw, from which there are superb views of the same scenery described by Southey from the vantage point of Crosthwaite Vicarage. Hardie could not ignore the issue. To the nature-impoverished dwellers of Liverpool, Manchester and the industrial cotton towns, becoming an important part of Keswick's tourist trade, the loss of such vistas of Lakeland would be cause for considerable concern. Hardie decided to resuscitate the old Keswick and District Footpath Preservation Association, canvassing hoteliers, tradespeople and anyone else dependent on walkers and ramblers for their livelihood. He hoped that some enlightened landowners would join, but in the event this proved to be wishful thinking. Local clergy were left to provide ultimate respectability for the Association, and Hardie accepted an invitation to become President. A colleague, the Reverend W. Colville, was elected vice-president.

Months of negotiation followed. Unfortunately, Mrs Spencer-Bell of Fawe Park, one of the offending estate owners, lost her son in a drowning accident. This rather cut the ground from under Hardie's feet, as he could hardly bring pressure to bear on one of his own parishioners in these circumstances.

By the autumn of 1886, anyone testing the right of access to Latrigg would find their way blocked by locked gates, barbed wire, newly-planted larch trees and a 'surly watcher', who turned ramblers back towards Keswick. At Fawe Park, the estate gates were regularly locked and sometimes barricaded with brambles and faggots. The policy Hardie advocated in an article on footpath preservation which he contributed to the *Contemporary Review* that year – 'every reasonable effort [should be made] to preserve ancient rights of way' – was patently having no effect.[38] Even 'pace-egging' was no longer to be allowed on its traditional site. 'On Easter Monday in the Keswick Valley', Hardie wrote, 'the children used always to go with their parents to the top of Latrigg ... to "trundle the eggs".'[39] In the Spring of 1887 some local lads were arrested and taken before the magistrate. They were let off on the understanding that some more responsible party would test the right of access to the top of the fell.

From then on battle was joined. Legend has it that the Vicar of Crosthwaite, crowbar in hand, at the head of an army of demon-strators variously estimated in hundreds or thousands, led a charge upon the barricades.[40] The truth, however, is somewhat different.

The first 'attack' on the blocked paths was made on 30 August 1887. A small party consisting only of the leaders of the Footpath Association assembled in front of the George Hotel in Keswick. They proceeded to Fawe Park, where they found Mrs Spencer-Bell waiting for them. She berated them at length but did not prevent them removing the obstacles which barred the right of way across her estate to Nichol Landing. On the same day, the footpath 'storm troopers' set off up Latrigg, expecting more effective opposition. They were not disappointed. Across the path was a colossal assem-blage of iron, wood and barbed wire, all freshly coated with tar. A lawyer, who had spun out months of negotiations on behalf of Mr J. J. Spedding, the estate owner, looked on with satisfaction as they tried in vain to pick a way through the barrier. He failed to see that in arranging for such a humiliation he might severely prejudice his client's case. When the news got out, and the landowners tried to brand the 'trespass' the work of a few agitators, both the Keswick tourist traders and the ramblers of the north-west united as one body. The temperature of the dispute rose dramatically.

Towards the end of September an orderly and determined crowd of between 400 and 500 people, led by the guide-book author H. I. Jenkinson, secretary and treasurer of the Association, invaded Fawe Park. Three days later, on 1 October, over 2,000 demonstrators lined up behind Radical MP Samuel Plimsoll at the foot of Latrigg. In the company of twelve men bearing crowbars, pickaxes and spades – the offer of a brass band was for some reason refused – they broke through a locked gate, unheeding of the now impotent lawyer's cries of 'trespass', and forged their way to the summit of the hill. Once there, they broke into a patriotic rendering of 'Rule Britannia'. For days afterwards, gangs of youths walked over Latrigg to keep the path open, chanting as they went:

The Lions of Keswick will break every chain,
And open the footpaths, again and again![41]

The Vicar of Crosthwaite was nowhere to be seen. He had not been seen at any of these demonstrations.

Hardie had been unsparing of his efforts to generate support for the Footpath Association. He lectured on footpath preservation to meetings in London, Oxford, Manchester, Liverpool, Birmingham and Bristol – wherever he could command an audience. He was highly sensitive to the critical relationship between landowner and rambler. The rules of the Association laid down that members should not only work for the preservation and maintenance of paths and verges, but also prevent damage to trees and crops, the disturbance of game and the carelessness of gates left open and discarded litter.[42]

In order to have some respite from the stress of all this campaigning which, combined with his parish work, was making him ill, he spent the early part of 1887 travelling in Europe on an extended period of leave. No sooner was he back in Keswick, however, than he was caught up once again in a maelstrom of activity. He was asked to co-ordinate the organisation of great bonfires which were to burn on beacons and mountain-tops throughout the kingdom in celebration of Queen Victoria's Golden Jubilee. Since the days of the Armada, national triumphs had been celebrated in this way, and in Wordsworth's time bonfires were lit nationwide to mark the victory at Waterloo. The preparations completely absorbed Hardie, and he could scarcely have been unaware of their significance at a period when many old beacon sites had been fenced off and barred to the public. On the clear summer evening of 22 June, 400 people climbed the 3,000-foot pinnacle of Skiddaw to set light to an enormous pyre of paraffin-soaked peats. In the distance could be seen 'no less than a hundred and forty-eight fires gleaming like diamond points on mountain heights and littoral plain. After the singing of the National Anthem the Vicar was seized and carried shoulder-high by the cheering crowd.'[43]

As the focus of enormous popular feeling, in relation to the footpaths dispute, Hardie was now in what seemed to him an impossible position. Should he, or should he not, involve himself in direct action? At the crucial planning meeting in Keswick's Court building on the night before the confrontation with Mrs Spencer-Bell, the Reverend W. Colville was obliged to take the chair. He expressed himself sorry at the absence of the President, 'who is so fertile and expedient in his remarks, and able to say the right thing'. Next day, on the barricades at Fawe Park, another Committee member, Routh Fitzpatrick, was heard to say in his argument with Mrs

Spencer-Bell: 'I am very sorry that the Association is not represented by our worthy President, as he would have been better able
to explain matters.' One dissentient voice at this point was heard to
shout 'No!' 'I am sorry', Fitzpatrick went on, 'but unfortunately he
is away from home.' Mrs Spencer-Bell suggested in reply that the
absent vicar should 'stick to preaching and not be a politician'.[44]

Just what vital business had called Hardie away at that time is a
mystery. Despite the legend, it seems that he was not prepared to
risk his reputation participating in any of the footpath demonstrations, however much he might agitate behind the scenes.

Writs for damages were issued against eight members of the
Keswick and District Footpath Preservation Association, and an
injunction to prevent further trespass was applied for by the owner
of Latrigg. The Association elected for trial by jury. The case was
heard at Carlisle Assizes and on 5 July 1888, at the close of the
defendants' evidence, a compromise was reached. The matter was
settled by consent, and the right of access to the top of Latrigg was
established.

Reverberations from the Keswick demonstrations were felt
halfway across the Irish Sea. On 17 October, according to the *Isle of
Man Examiner*, barely two weeks after the mass 'trespass' on
Latrigg, a footpath committee in Peel concluded that the time was
ripe to re-open the right of way to Creg Malin headlands. They

> decided that the best plan would be to follow the example
> of the people of Keswick ... 400 persons, comprising
> fishermen and a number of tradesmen, and some women
> assembled on the marine parade ... The procession then
> started for the headlands with members of the committee
> leading ... they came to the boundary of Mr. Cain's
> property. Here they were met by Mr. Cain (the owner) and
> Mr. T. Kneen, advocate [from] Douglas, who was retained
> by him. Four members of the committee ... climbed over
> the hedge into the pathway ... Mr. Kneen confronted
> them ... then became somewhat excited, and indulged in
> an angry altercation with the committee, and especially
> with Mr. Kermode. The latter gentleman, on being informed
> by Kneen that he was not worth powder and shot, replied
> to the learned counsel that *he* came there to represent a
> sneak and a coward. Mr. M. A. Collister put an end to the
> unseemly affair by remarking, 'What's the use of listening
> to all this; let us move forward.' The procession, which
> had kept in order with wonderful patience, followed the

committee along the direction where the pathway had
been. It ... had been ploughed up in both this and the
neighbouring fields, and in one of them had been sown
with turnips.[45]

Notwithstanding the turnips, the procession won through, and the
footpath was liberated.

Still the moving spirit of the Lake District Defence Society, Hardie
had a full schedule and everywhere he went there were reminders
of work to be done: a threat of quarrying on Loughrigg to be investigated; a campaign to be mounted to forestall the closure of public
access to Stock Ghyll Force; a case to be made against the Barrow
Waterworks scheme to dam the River Duddon, the Duddon to
which Wordsworth addressed no less than 34 of his sonnets.

Manchester Corporation was making an increasingly unsightly
mess of the fellsides around Thirlmere. It was beginning to dawn
on people that soon they would have to say goodbye for ever to the
quiet footpaths threading the Wythburn Valley which Matthew
Arnold had described in his poem *Resignation*. The new road on the
eastern shore of the reservoir was an 'improvement' the LDDS
fiercely opposed, but without success. The famous 'Rock of
Names' was dynamited. Situated halfway between Dove Cottage
and Greta Hall, the home of Southey, the rock had been the trysting
place of the Wordsworths, William's fiancée Mary Hutchinson and
her sister, and Samuel Taylor Coleridge. They had carved their
initials on it, and over the years it had become an object of venera-
tion by admirers of the Lake poets. Few sights were more pathetic
than that of Hardie and Edith searching for two days in the rubble,
piecing together fragments of the rock which they restored in the
form of a cairn above the new road, where it remained for almost a
century. In 1984 the cairn was removed in highly questionable
circumstances. The pieces were 'restored' and are now to be found
set in a rock face at the back of the Wordsworth Museum in Grasmere.

In the autumn of 1888 the new Cumberland County Council was
formed. Hardie stood for election in the Keswick division as an
Independent Liberal, and topped the poll. During his period as a
councillor he was the driving force behind many new projects. In
addition to his commitment to education, he was concerned with
organic farming methods, preventing the pollution of rivers with
mining spoil, and ensuring that footpaths were properly sign-

The opening ceremony at Brandelhow Park on Derwentwater, 16 October 1902. The ceremony was performed by Princess Louise, who had helped Octavia Hill and Canon Rawnsley with the Trust's first major appeal in the Lake District. (NT)

Canon Rawnsley was often invited to preside over meetings, lectures and fêtes in the Lake District. Here he is depicted in 1913 in a pen and crayon sketch by an unknown artist, at the Grasmere Sports, prepared for rain under a huge black umbrella. (By permission of Rosalind Rawnsley)

Sir Robert Hunter in 1907. He served as Chairman of the National Trust from its foundation until his death in 1913. (NT)

(Opposite) *Mass trespass: Manchester ramblers setting off for Kinder Scout in the Peak District on 24 April 1932. Footpath demonstrations at Keswick and Creg Malin had been forceful and peaceful, but this excursion onto the Derbyshire grouse moors provoked a fracas with gamekeepers and the ringleaders were prosecuted and imprisoned. (NT)*

The President of the Norfolk and Norwich Naturalists' Society, Russell Colman, handing over the deeds of Scolt Head to Viscount Ullswater, Vice-President of the National Trust, thus providing the site as a nature reserve, 11 June 1923. (NT)

Miraculously the pilot escaped with only a minor head injury, having crashed his bi-plane on Blakeney Point in Norfolk during the vegetation survey of 25 July 1922. (NT)

(Below) *The Levant Engine House on the West Penwith coast of Cornwall, in a photograph taken in 1904. In 1967 this site of industrial archaeology was given to the National Trust with help from the local authority, the Cornish Engines Preservation Society, and a public appeal. (NT)*

Major Lawrence Johnston with some of his favourite dachshunds, on the Theatre Lawn of Hidcote Manor in Gloucestershire. The famous garden at Hidcote, containing plants collected by Major Johnston from many parts of the world, was the first garden to be acquired by the National Trust in 1948 under the National Gardens Scheme. (NT)

Philip Kerr, 11th Marquess of Lothian, from a drawing by A. de B. Footner. Kerr was very much the moving force behind the Country Houses Scheme and the National Trust Act of 1937. His own estate, Blickling in Norfolk, passed to the Trust in 1940. (NT)

Wightwick Manor in the West Midlands, the first property donated to the National Trust under the Country Houses Scheme, whereby the Trust could acquire and hold land or investments as endowments for the upkeep of great houses. (NT)

The tenants' meeting in the Great Hall at Cotehele in Cornwall in 1947, at which Lord Mount Edgcumbe announced that his medieval house and lands on the River Tamar were to be transferred to the National Trust. (NT)

The National Trust continues the battle to preserve open spaces. This poster by David Gentleman showing the line of a proposed by-pass through the park of Petworth House in Sussex, was printed in 1975 as part of the Trust's campaign to save the landscape designed by 'Capability' Brown and made famous in Turner's paintings. (NT)

posted and maintained. As chairman of Highways and Bridges he vehemently opposed plans for the construction of roads over the high Lakeland passes. His attitude to the region was controversial but far-sighted. He objected to the installation of overhead telegraph wires in Borrowdale and the granting of new liquor licences in Keswick.

> The ring of his nailed boots on the cobbles outside, claimed
> one county councillor, struck dismay into many a council's
> heart, heralding as it did the imminent appearance of a
> stocky, charming but wonderfully alert cleric with
> penetrating eyes and a beard that could bristle![46]

His persistence and single-minded determination made him not a few enemies. Having offended a number of people with vested interests, and refusing to compromise his ideals, Hardie failed to be re-elected. The *West Cumberland Times* records how

> In 1895 Rawnsley was opposed by Mr. R. D. Marshall, who
> received 525 votes to the 400 recorded for his opponent ...
> According to a quatrain of the time [certainly by Hardie]
>   'Lies and liquor defeated the Vicar,
>   Which none of us need surprise;
>   But 400 wise, think that liquor and lies
>   Will bring vengeance on Keswick the quicker.'
> Something other than lies and liquor cause defeat. The
> foregoing verse, for instance. It was reported that when
> the County Council met, Rawnsley would have been
> appointed an alderman but for those lines.[47]

At the farewell party on his leaving office, Hardie's role as Lakeland's most energetic publicist was recognised. He continued this work by devoting himself to writing a series of books extolling the beauty, the life and the customs of the region. The first of these, *A Coach-drive at the Lakes* (1890), amalgamates three articles originally written for the *Cornhill Magazine* and describes the road from Windermere to Keswick, discussing interesting features on the way, and ending the journey in the KSIA souvenir shop. The back of the book carried advertisements for the LDDS and the Footpath Association; also a country code, urging visitors to keep to the paths, show respect for the flora and fauna, keep their dogs on leads and shut the gates. Among the later books, two are still of outstanding interest: *Literary Associations of the English Lakes* (1894) contains much that is not recorded elsewhere in the story of English literature, and *Months at the Lakes* (1906) comprises a calendar of traditions in the region, many of which survive to the present day.

In the winter of 1890 Hardie had suffered a mild heart attack and was ordered to take a complete break. He saw this as an opportunity for a three-month excursion down the Nile, recording everything, for yet another book. The sight of the Pyramids on this journey transmuted his love of history into an obsession with memorials. On his return to England his mind was focused almost exclusively on this subject. During the following two years he erected a runic cross on the lower slopes of Skiddaw in memory of two sheep farmers, an inscribed stone at Wythburn Church to recall its association with Matthew Arnold, and with Frances Power Cobbe, a pioneer of the anti-vivisection movement, he erected a memorial slab on Helvellyn.[48] This stone records the faithful devotion of a terrier who for three months guarded the body of her master, a young Manchester fell-walker who had fallen to his death from Striding Edge in the Spring of 1805.

A fountain at Cockermouth dedicated to William and Dorothy Wordsworth, a stone cross 40 feet high to the memory of the poet Caedmon at Whitby, a monument at Roker Point, Sunderland to the Venerable Bede, and an inscription of his own sonnet in praise of the Mawddach on a cliff at Barmouth are among the enduring landmarks for which Hardie was responsible.

Perhaps a reason for this obsession was that the generation which had moulded Hardie's character and ideals was gradually passing away. Thring died in the autumn of 1887, Bishop Goodwin in 1891, his mother in May of the following year, and Dr Jowett a year later. Lewis Nettleship, a constant friend and near contemporary, died from exposure during a climb on Mont Blanc in 1892. The following summer, Hardie went to Chamonix to discover from the guides how the tragedy had happened.

On 16 November 1893, Hardie was in London. With Bob Hunter and Octavia Hill he was at a meeting to discuss the formation of the National Trust for Historic Sites and Natural Scenery. Six days later he returned to the north for his installation as a Canon of Carlisle Cathedral. He could scarcely have envisaged at that time that rather than 'Defender of the Lake District', he would become known to future generations as 'Canon Rawnsley of the National Trust'.

CHAPTER 5

The Birth of the National Trust

Prior to the foundation of the National Trust, although open spaces in and near towns and cities had become the concern of municipal authorities, and in some places historic buildings also, there was no national organisation which could realise the growing concern for the preservation of unspoilt privately-owned landscape and places of historical interest. Increasing mobility and prosperity in the Victorian era had made even the remotest parts of the country-side accessible to a greater number of people than ever before. As a result, there was a corresponding increase in pressure to create an effective means of protecting rural beauty from the depredations of developers, and the insensitive exploitation of its resources.

The Commons Preservation Society had come into existence in direct response to the prospect that all common land would one day be enclosed, built over in urban areas, and made inaccessible to the public in areas of agricultural improvement. The preserva-tion of open spaces was the reason for its foundation, and the defence of common rights was the means by which it prosecuted that aim. By the 1880s the CPS realised that a policy strictly limited to the defence of common rights was not an adequate means of furthering its true purpose. Under Octavia Hill and Robert Hunter's influence, the Society broadened its area of concern to include the defence of rights of way, and in conjunction with the Kyrle Society actively promoted the preservation of beautiful countryside, whether common land or land in private ownership. Threats to scenery and footpaths in the Lake District and around London had largely been responsible for bringing about this change of policy. In 1899 the CPS incorporated the National Foot-paths Society and eleven years later was renamed the Commons,

Open Spaces and Footpaths Preservation Society.

Preservation and conservation in the countryside had also been the concern of various Societies of Antiquaries since the end of the eighteenth century. Among their achievements was the passing of the Ancient Monuments Act in 1882, which protected prehistoric earthworks, megalithic remains, dolmens, stone circles including Stonehenge, stone avenues and tumuli. Eighteen years later, provision was made for the protection of certain limited categories of ancient buildings and ruins.[1] Old buildings of architectural merit or national interest, however, remained outside the scope of this legislation.

On 5 March 1877 in a letter to the *Athenaeum* William Morris highlighted the possible fate of unprotected buildings by drawing attention to Sir Gilbert Scott's drastic 'restoration' of Tewkesbury Abbey. As a result of his letter, the Society for the Protection of Ancient Buildings (SPAB) came into being 17 days later.

Ruskin, in his *Seven Lamps of Architecture* (1849) had been the first to attack the confidence of restorers:

> It is impossible, as impossible as to raise the dead, to restore
> anything that has ever been great or beautiful in archi-
> tecture ... Do not let us talk then of restoration. The
> thing is a lie from beginning to end ... that spirit which
> is given only by the hand and eye of the workman can never
> be recalled.[2]

He valued the surface of buildings, both for the patina of age and the unique marks of the original craftsmen. The fashion for reproducing structures with machine-powered tools destroyed both the weathered beauty of the original and the record of craft and usage laid down on wood and stone. In place of proper repair and maintenance, restoration had become a euphemism for rebuilding and faking. The importance of preserving original surfaces in addition to maintaining structures earned the SPAB its nickname of 'Anti-Scrape'.

Within six years the SPAB was transformed from a pressure group, dominated by protesting artists, into a repository of knowledge and experience for architects whose particular interest was old building styles and techniques. It was described in 1924 by Professor William Lethaby, one of its leading architects, as 'a school of rational builders'.[3]

Like the Societies of Antiquaries, the SPAB was not constituted to own ancient ruins or old buildings. It was only able to offer advice where advice was sought. Its sphere of influence remained small, confined to wealthy property-owners who were aware of its existence, and sympathetic to its aims, or to trustees who had been specifically appointed to manage historic buildings.

The seventeenth-century manor house of Sayes Court, Deptford, now demolished, would have benefited from the SPAB's advice on restoration and maintenance, had funds been available to carry out its recommendations. In 1884 its elderly owner, Mr W. J. Evelyn, intimated to Octavia Hill that he wished to make a gift of the house and its surrounding land for the enjoyment of the public. Bob Hunter was asked to prepare a report. He concluded that the local authority would have no statutory power to use public funds to maintain the house, were they to accept it. The only alternative would be the cumbersome procedure of a trusteeship, which would be invalidated should the donor die within the year. This realisation prompted Bob Hunter to write to Octavia Hill suggesting the formation of a Land Company, to hold properties in the public interest. Her response was enthusiastic. 'I think such a Company as you suggest would be valuable ...'

The idea had come too late to secure Sayes Court, but Octavia was aware that 'at any moment some other important scheme may present itself and our body ought to be ready'. At the time, she described herself as 'very low in spirits seeing so much work I ought to do and having nothing like time to deal with it. It will be a great comfort to think this scheme of the Company is prospering.'[4]

The next month, Bob Hunter sent a paper to the National Association of Social Science, meeting in Birmingham, entitled 'A Suggestion for the Better Preservation of Open Spaces'. In it he pointed out that manors comprising private and common land were coming onto the market with increasing frequency. There was a danger that, under pressure to raise the value of their estates, landowners would initiate a fresh wave of legal enclosures. 'Since a voluntary association cannot buy land and become a commoner' there was but one course of action available:

> the formation of a corporate company under the Joint Stock Companies' Acts for the following purposes: To acquire properties possessing common rights; to manage all open spaces acquired in the public interest; to co-operate with local authorities for the laying out of public gardens; and to exercise, for protection of open spaces, rights of common attached to properties purchased. Such a company might make considerable income from properties acquired, and

its operations might be general or local. The central idea of this is that of a Land Company which shall administer its property with a view to the protection of the public interests in open spaces.[5]

He sent several copies of this paper to Octavia Hill for distribution to friends and sympathisers. Like Bob Hunter, she saw the proposition principally as a means of increasing the provision of urban and rural open spaces for public enjoyment; the preservation of historic buildings was a secondary consideration. In February she replied:

Thank you for the circular, which I shall endeavour to place as opportunity offers.
A short expressive name is difficult to find for the new Company. What do you think of 'The Commons and Garden Trust' – and then printing in small letters – 'for accepting, holding and purchasing open space for the people in town and country'? I do not know that I am right in thinking that it would be called a Trust. But if it would, I think it might be better than 'Company' – you will do better, I believe to bring forward its benevolent than its commercial character.[6]

Bob Hunter pencilled at the top of this letter '? National Trust R.H.'
A few weeks later, representatives of the Kyrle Society and the CPS met at the home of James Bryce to consider the proposal. Nothing came of the discussion, however, as Shaw-Lefevre feared that a new conservation body would take support away from the older amenity societies. He correctly forecast the eclipse of the CPS should the 'National Trust' come into being.
At the time these exchanges were taking place, Octavia Hill, Shaw-Lefevre and Baroness Burdett-Coutts had formed a Hampstead Heath Extension Committee under the chairmanship of the Duke of Westminster. A scheme to preserve the privately-owned lands of East Park and Parliament Hill Fields as an extension to the Heath was proposed to the local authorities. A thousand dignitaries attended a grand garden party on Parliament Hill, where to the accompaniment of music from the band of the Coldstream Guards, they were invited to tour the proposed extension.
The occasion was a brilliant flop. The owners, Lord Mansfield and Sir Spencer Maryon Wilson, were asking over £300,000 for the land. It was only when Shaw-Lefevre and Bob Hunter drafted an enabling Bill for Parliament to authorise its purchase by local

authorities that 'for very shame of seeing a voluntary body taking responsibility for London's affairs', the Metropolitan Board and local Vestries promised substantial sums of money. Octavia was left to raise £52,500 by public subscription, a target achieved in eight months. The land came into the Board's possession in March 1889.

The present-day wild appearance of Hampstead Heath is largely due to the stinginess of the Board, who rather than spend ratepayers' money on shrubberies and 'municipal dahlias' scattered gorse seed 'because it was cheaper'. 'Posterity gained the most convincing illusion ever created of real country brought to the heart of a vast city'.[7]

Octavia Hill was at this time also assisting Millicent Fawcett in a similar fund-raising operation to secure The Lawns, the Fawcett's former home now called Vauxhall Park, and Hilly Fields, a recreation ground in Lewisham. In the Lake District, Hardie Rawnsley was appointed one of the trustees responsible for the maintenance of Dove Cottage, the home of Wordsworth. This form of management had already been established over Milton's cottage, purchased by the inhabitants of Chalfont St Giles in 1887, and various Shakespearian properties in Stratford-upon-Avon. The Reverend Stopford Brooke, having been given an option to buy Dove Cottage for £650, launched an appeal which raised £1,000. The cottage was restored to the condition in which the Wordsworths had known it 80 years before, and opened to the public in 1892.

Bob Hunter's suggestion meanwhile had not been forgotten. In 1893 several important sites in the Lake District came up for sale, among them the island on Grasmere and the celebrated Falls of Lodore. The CPS could no longer withstand pressure for the creation of an organisation specifically constituted to prevent the insensitive exploitation of rural properties where there was no hope of purchase by the local authorities. A fringe of villas already extended along the shores of Windermere and there was an immediate danger of further building round other lakes. Tollgates to waterfalls were also in prospect.

Shaw-Lefevre withdrew his objections. A preliminary meeting to discuss the formation of a 'National Trust for Historic Sites and Natural Scenery' was called by Bob Hunter, Octavia Hill and Hardie Rawnsley. In an office at the headquarters of the CPS on 16 November, as *The Times* reported a day later, the new association was brought into being to act as general trustees for all property intended for the use and enjoyment of the nation at large. Its function is to accept from private owners of property gifts of places of interest or beauty which can only be made if a perpetual custodian and administrator can be found.

The Trust was to be incorporated under the Joint Stock Companies Acts with licence, because of its non-profit-making status, to dispense with the use of the word 'Limited' in its title. It was foreseen that it might eventually require 'a Royal Charter or a Special Act of Parliament'; in any event it would need 'powers to make and enforce bylaws'. 'Persons who have no desirable property to hand over may be moved to endow [the Trust] with funds for the purchase of such property from others ... the association should endeavour to stimulate the generosity of well-to-do people.' The writer of *The Times* report, who was probably Bob Hunter, went on to suggest that the Trust might in certain circumstances seek powers of compulsory purchase: 'We see no reason why for public purposes a bit of beautiful scenery should not be the subject of a forced sale under equitable conditions just as much as a bit of ugly country for a railway.'

Five months later a second preliminary meeting approved a Memorandum and Articles of Association for the new company.

In view of his active role on the Hampstead Heath Extension Committee and the support he had shown to the Kyrle Society, it was agreed that the Duke of Westminster should be invited to become President of the National Trust. He had represented Chester in the House of Commons for 22 years, succeeding his father as Marquis of Westminster in 1869. Having been a loyal supporter of Gladstone's first administration, he was offered a dukedom, but later showed his independence by signing a manifesto of dissent to government policy in 1885. With a private fortune based on 600 acres of property in London and a 30,000-acre estate on the borders of Cheshire and Flintshire, Westminster would inspire confidence in those who might endow the fledgling Trust with land and legacies. Once he had accepted the presidency, the inaugural meeting took place under his chairmanship in Grosvenor House on Monday 16 July 1894.

Robert Hunter and Octavia Hill had for the previous three years been compiling a list of eminent people to serve on the Trust Council. Members of the aristocracy, nominees from the old universities, the Provost of Eton and Members of Parliament were included. Representatives of various organisations which might be useful to the Trust were also to be invited: the Linnean Society, the Royal Academy of Arts (Sir Frederick Leighton) the London Society of Antiquaries, the Royal Institute of British Architects, the SPAB, the Royal Botanic Society, the County Councils Association and the Trustees of Public Reservations in the USA. The CPS and the Kyrle Society were represented by Shaw-Lefevre and Harriot Yorke respectively. Of the artists Holman Hunt, George Frederick Watts and Walter Crane who attended the inaugural meeting, Watts was later elected.

Today the Council is reviewed on a regular basis and its composition changed if necessary to include representation from a wider range of social, political and environmental interests, as occurred recently. Given the circumstances of its foundation, however, it is perhaps not surprising that for many years the National Trust's management was not more broadly based in terms of social background. Octavia Hill wanted

> men and women who should be free from the tendency to
> sacrifice ... treasures to mercenary considerations, or to
> vulgarise them in accordance with popular cries – should
> be, in fact, those to whom historic memories loom large,
> who love the wild bird, butterfly, and plant, who realise the
> national value of hill slope lighted by sun or shadowed by
> cloud. So the governing body is nominated by the great
> artistic, learned, and scientific foundations of the United
> Kingdom.[8]

It is a pity that class prejudice excluded tenants of her housing schemes, some of whom could certainly have made a useful contribution to the council.

The balance of nominated members has always been weighted in favour of the preservation of property over access. John Bailey, who was Trust chairman in the late 1920s, made this perfectly plain. 'Preservation', he said, 'may always permit of access, while without preservation access becomes for ever impossible.'[9] The anxiety in the Trust which gave rise to such statements was first expressed at the 1894 inaugural meeting by Lord Carlisle, representing the Trustees of the National Gallery.

> Sometimes a well-meaning landowner, in his endeavour to
> give access to a beautiful spot, spoilt the whole country.
> Thus the society might also act as an educator. The only
> tourist to whom he objected was the one who carried a
> trowel ...

Nowadays the problem is not so much the trowel, as landowners who plough up footpaths and thereby help to increase the sheer weight of numbers on Trust land.

The inaugural meeting passed two constitutional resolutions. The first was moved by Octavia Hill:

> it is desirable to provide means by which landowners and others may be enabled to dedicate to the nation places of historic interest or natural beauty, and that for this purpose it is expedient to form a corporate body, capable of holding land, and representative of national institutions and interests.

The Trust should not only preserve ancient ruins and beautiful landscapes, she went on to say, but also substantial buildings such as the English manor house. A second resolution, moved by Bob Hunter, authorised the taking of necessary steps 'to procure the legal incorporation of the Trust'. This was achieved in January of the following year.

Hardie Rawnsley was appointed Honorary Secretary, a position he held for 26 years, until his death in 1920. *The Times* report of his speech at the inaugural meeting is peppered with acclamations:

> There was no society which could do the work which the Trust proposed for itself ... They were really establishing a great National Gallery of natural pictures. (Cheers) The dormant sense of the beautiful was awakening in the mass of our population, and this association would, it was hoped, do much to rouse it to activity. But for such action as was contemplated many a lovely bit of English landscape would be irretrievably ruined. (Cheers)[10]

The first Executive Committee meeting was held in February the following year. It established a pattern of leadership which would hold good for the first 16 years of the National Trust's existence and its steady acquisition of property. Bob Hunter had been elected Chairman, Harriot Yorke, Honorary Treasurer, and Octavia Hill was made responsible for appeals. Lawrence Chubb, who had been observed as a keen young student at the London Polytechnic by Bob Hunter, was appointed paid secretary. His real interests lay in commons and footpaths, and after a year he left to become secretary of the CPS. The Duke of Westminster, Edmund Maurice, Herbert Goss of the Entomological Society, Rutter Fletcher of the SPAB, and the architect Alfred Waterhouse were all active on the first committee. Co-opted in later years were Hardie Rawnsley's brother Willingham, a master at Uppingham and author of the *Highways and Byways Guide to Lincolnshire* (1914) and Bob Hunter's daughter Dorothy, who went on to serve as an elected member from 1934 to 1966.

Within a short time of the inaugural meeting, Hardie Rawnsley announced that he had arranged for the acquisition of the Trust's first property. Dinas Oleu, 'the Fortress of Light', a four-and-a-half acre rectangle of rough grazing enclosed by dry-stone walls, forms part of the magnificent cliff above the small Welsh seaport of Barmouth at the mouth of the Mawddach estuary. It was owned by Fanny Talbot, an old friend of Hardie's, and might have been given to the Guild of St George had she not become disillusioned with Ruskin. A few years previously Mrs Talbot had donated a row of old cottages below Dinas Oleu to the Guild for a co-operative housing scheme. Ruskin visited her once, but despite his love of Welsh vernacular architecture and Mrs Talbot's pleas that he should return, he refused to become involved in the day-to-day affairs of Welsh cottagers.[11] Reached by stone stairs and tracks hidden between the old houses of the town, Dinas Oleu commands a magnificent view over Cardigan Bay.

The July 1896 National Trust Report shows a large number of properties under consideration. The executive did not just wait for gifts like Dinas Oleu to fall into its lap. As well as open spaces, the sites of ancient earthworks and monuments, houses associated with famous artists and writers were all investigated. The purchase of Coleridge's cottage, in the village of Nether Stowey in Somerset, was being negotiated by a local committee, although it did not come into the possession of the Trust until 1909.

A half-timbered Clergy House at Alfriston on the Sussex Downs, probably the earliest surviving of its type in the south of England, was the first building that the Trust acquired. For several years the local vicar had been campaigning for its restoration and the house was almost a ruin when the SPAB recommended a London architect to supervise its rescue. Unfortunately, anonymous criticism in the press, saying that such an expense was not justified 'since there is nothing to do but replace rotten timbers and generally repair' provoked him to resign. The SPAB then alerted the National Trust, who immediately negotiated purchase of the property from the Ecclesiastical Commissioners in the winter of 1896. The price was a nominal £10.

In places, the thatched roof was open to the sky, rain

streamed through, unhindered, to the rooms below.
Several walls bulged ominously; within, the staircase leading
to the upper floor had entirely disappeared. It stood a
forlorn relic.[12]

Octavia began an appeal for £350, the estimated cost of repairs. For
this work she considered it essential to procure someone 'who
could be there himself, whose heart was in the matter and who
could decide point by point on the spot what to do and see to its
being done, with knowledge of art and craft.' The SPAB now
recommended Alfred Powell, another architect with a good
knowledge of medieval craft skills.[13] By January 1897 he had
succeeded in making the building secure and the roof ready for re-
thatching that spring.

Attention was next drawn to the plight of 15 acres of cliff top on
the north Cornish coast near the village of Tintagel. The land,
known as Barras Head, was in danger of being sold for hotel building. It overlooks a dramatic outcrop of rock on which stand the
ruins of King Arthur's castle. Thanks to the power of Arthurian
romance, the £505 needed to buy the site was raised within five
months. The Trust later acquired the nearby Tintagel Old Post
Office, a picturesque fourteenth-century house, for £200.

Spurred on by the success of the Barras Head appeal, the Trust
secured a loan for the acquisition of the sixteenth-century Joiners'
Hall in Salisbury, a small building with an interesting half-
timbered facade. In 1899, a small part of Wicken Fen was
purchased for £10. Described in the Annual Report as 'almost the
last remnant of primaeval fenland', it had fortunately escaped the
attentions of Roman and Dutch drainage engineers, and was
prized by naturalists as the habitat of rare plants and butterflies.
While the wind and steam pumps of East Anglia dried out all that
was left of the 2,500 square miles of the Great Level, the Trust
bought more and more strips of Wicken Fen, until the country's
first nature reserve encompassed 700 acres of wetland.

Following the example of the Trustees of American Reservations, Octavia Hill devised a scheme by means of which land could
be given in memory of friends or relatives. Toys Hill on the edge of
the Kentish Weald was the first landholding to be acquired in this
way. During the First World War the Trust urged individuals and
organisations to consider the possibility of dedicating open spaces
to commemorate those who died in the service of their country.
Among lands given in response to this appeal were the crest of
Scafell Pike, in memory of the men of the Lake District, and over

1,000 acres of the Scafell range, with Great End and Great Gable; a tribute to members of the Fell and Rock Climbing Club. Hardie Rawnsley gave a viewpoint in Borrowdale, which he named 'Peace How', in memory of the men of Keswick.

While Octavia Hill went on to capture the tops of the Kentish Weald, including Ide Hill and Mariner's Hill, a committee under the guidance of Bob Hunter raised funds for the purchase of beauty spots in the vicinity of his home in Haslemere: 750 acres of Hindhead Common, including the Devil's Punchbowl, was presented to the Trust in 1906 by the Hindhead Preservation Committee. It was the first of a score of open spaces amounting to more than 2,000 acres in that locality, acquired during the following 16 years.

The death of Ruskin at Brantwood on 20 January 1900 occasioned the Trust's first appeal in the Lake District. As a tribute to his inspiration, Hardie Rawnsley suggested the erection of a memorial to the man whose ideas had stimulated the founders' appreciation of nature and architecture. Two years before his death, Ruskin had sent through Hardie a conciliatory message to Octavia Hill, breaking the silence that had lasted between them for 20 years. The memorial to Ruskin, a monolith of Borrowdale slate bearing a bronze medallion portrait, was erected on Friars Crag above Derwent Water, on land which was later to be bought by subscription as a memorial to Hardie himself. Here Ruskin had been taken at the age of five, and later recorded what he described as

The first thing which I remember, as an event in life ...
the intense joy, mingled with awe, that I had in looking
through the hollows in the mossy roots, over the crag into
the dark lake, [it] has ever associated itself more or less
with all twining roots of trees ever since.[14]

The first of the Lake District land appeals was launched within a year and a half of the unveiling of the Ruskin memorial. Brandlehow Park Estate, over 100 acres on the western shore of Derwent Water, was offered to the Trust for £6,500, provided the purchase price could be found within six months. In less than five months, fund-raising committees in Manchester, Liverpool, Leeds, Birmingham and Keswick collected £7,500. Many factory workers contributed to the appeal: not unusual was the donor describing himself simply as 'a working man', who sent two shillings, with a note expressing regret that he could not give more: 'I once saw

Derwent Water and can never forget it. I will do what I can to get my mates to help.'[15] *The Times* on the day of opening, described the scene as

> Washed by the waters of the Lake on the one side, on the other it is bounded by the open hillside of Cat Bells. Brandlehow carries rights of common on Cat Bells: and thus the purchase gives the public an interest in the whole side of the lake from the shore to the summit of the hill. The estate possesses all the characteristics of Derwent Water scenery. Sloping down to the water steeply, but not abruptly, one of its most charming features is a tract of open meadow falling in varied curves to Southey's 'mutton-pie' bay, and carrying fine trees of many kinds ... The experiment of managing a tract of woodland for purposes of pleasure in the interests, not of the proprietor, but of the public, and with a view both to the enjoyment of the wood itself and to its appearance from the lake, is an interesting one, and may well exercise the ingenuity of the National Trust and its advisers ... It is to be hoped that the precedent, set in a conspicuous manner by the acquisition of Brandlehow, may be followed both on other waters of the Lake District and in other parts of the country, and that the nation may gradually acquire such an interest in its more beautiful places of resort as to put them out of danger from the operation of passing private interest.

Brandlehow was opened by Princess Louise on 16 October 1902 in the presence of the Trust's three founders. *The Times* report the next day made light of the inauspicious weather:

> The Princess, who is vice-president ... was accompanied by the Duke of Argyll, and arrived at Keswick from Lowther Castle, where they have been guests of Lord Lonsdale, who travelled with them. A crowd of people assembled outside of the railway station gave the party a cordial greeting as they entered the carriages and drove through the decorated streets ... After leaving the Market-square the party made a call at the Keswick School of Industrial Art, where the Princess, who was received by Mrs. Rawnsley, had an opportunity of inspecting a tablet recently executed there as a memorial of Queen Victoria. A move was then made, by way of Portinscale, to

Brandlehow, where a large crowd of people had assembled. The weather was wet and showery, but rain fortunately held off during the ceremony.

Octavia Hill wrote from Derwent Island later that day:

The scene was really most beautiful and very funnily primitive. The great tent was blown to atoms; and the little red dais was out under the free sky, with the great lake and splendid mountains, and golden bracken slopes around us; and the nice north country people quite near, and so happy and orderly. The Princess was most kind, and really deeply interested in the National Trust work.[16]

The Times went on:

Princess Louise was escorted to the platform, where Canon Rawnsley read an address, which contained a short history of the acquisition of the property and thanked her Royal Highness for coming to declare the park open. The address was enclosed in an ornamental silver casket, which had been wrought for the occasion by the Keswick School of Industrial Art. Mr. Mitchell Dawson, in the names of various committees ... presented to the Princess an album containing photographs of the lake and surrounding scenery, given by Mr. Pettitt [the photographer]. Her Royal Highness declared the park open ... A flag was hoisted, the band of the 1st V.B. the Border Regiment played the National Anthem, and the crowd raised an enthusiastic cheer.

Before leaving Brandlehow the Princess and the Duke of Argyll each planted an oak tree, and three other trees were afterwards planted by Miss Octavia Hill, Canon Rawnsley, and Sir John Hibbert [Chairman of Lancashire County Council. *The English Lakes Visitor*, 18 Oct., claims Bob Hunter planted the fifth tree].

Gowbarrow Park, with Aira Force, near the site of Wordsworth's 'host, of golden daffodils', was the Trust's next and much larger Lake District acquisition. In his book *Round the Lake Country* (1909) Hardie describes the waterfall:

... and watch the amber torrent turn to silver (for there

has been a heavy rain) as it flashes far down in its eighty-feet leap and casts upwards its rainbow spray and the sweet fragrance of its peat-brown water-flood.[17]

The fell, with its 750 acres of woodland and heather rising from the northern shores of Ullswater, would almost certainly have lost its lower slopes to villa-building but for this timely intervention. The asking price of £12,800 was appealed for through the nationwide fund-raising committees, with groups in Edinburgh, Newcastle and Sheffield added to their number. The first donor, according to Hardie, was a child in Glasgow, who gave him threepence after hearing him give a talk about the property.[18] Workers in the Lancashire cotton towns also contributed and artists donated paintings to be sold in aid of the appeal. A Trust leaflet went so far as to suggest that the government should nationalise the whole of the Lake District in order to prevent further house-building on this and other places of beauty.[19]

Gowbarrow Fell was opened to the public on 9 August 1906 by the Speaker of the House of Commons, J. W. Lowther, Lakeland's largest landowner. He congratulated the

sixteen hundred persons who had fallen victims to the solicitations of Canon Rawnsley and Miss Octavia Hill, and who had so generously and so unselfishly planked down the money, not for their own enjoyment altogether, but for that of their fellow citizens. We have all heard of the mountain in labour that brought forth a mouse, this time the mice have been in labour and have brought forth a mountain.[20]

In 1908 another 100 acres between Brandlehow and the River Derwent almost doubled the size of the National Trust's Derwent Water holding. Two years later were added 310 acres of Grange Fell with the Bowder Stone and the Borrowdale Birches, also bought by public subscription. There followed a steady succession of Lake District properties before 1913: Stybarrow Crag on Ullswater, Queen Adelaide's Hill overlooking Windermere, the 'Borrans Field' site of a Roman fort at Ambleside, the Druids' Circle near Keswick.

Those most directly involved in making the Lake District National Trust territory from the earliest years included Gordon Wordsworth (the poet's grandson), Gordon Somervell, Frank Marshall, Hugh Redmayne, Professor Collingwood of the

Cumberland and Westmorland Antiquarian and Archaeological Society, and Noël Rawnsley. It hardly needs saying that the most enthusiastic and active participant was, of course, Noël's ubiquitous father.

During the first quarter-century of the National Trust's existence, over 80 properties were acquired. Of these more than 60 were open spaces, including six stretches of coastline. The remainder included two manor houses and a dozen smaller historic buildings, two dovecotes and a series of bridges over the River Wey.

Not surprisingly, many of the open spaces were in the areas of the country not far from where the founders lived. Most of them were heath and woodland and all, except the eleven in the Lake District, were in the southern half of the country. A number of them were also the sites of prehistoric ruins and earthworks. The largest single acquisition was 7,000 acres of the Holnicote Estate in Somerset, leased and later given to the Trust. It was the property of Sir Charles Acland, a Liberal Member of Parliament, whose service on Lloyd-George's land enquiry had made him realise the immorality of personally owning vast acreages of the countryside. He offered Holnicote to the National Trust in a spirit of genuine philanthropy, for the benefit and enjoyment of the public. The most extensive of the coastlands was Blakeney Point in north Norfolk, approximately 1,100 acres of sand dunes, scrub and shingle which is the haunt of waders, oystercatchers, terns and rarer seabirds. The donors were to remain anonymous.

Of the Trust's early acquisitions it had often been said that they were accepted almost indiscriminately. This may have been true of some small and isolated open spaces, but it was certainly not so in the case of the modest-size buildings. All but one of these is now open to the public on a regular basis, and the majority attract a good many visitors. In the main, whatever the Trust accepted during the lifetime of the founders was well chosen.

In June 1918 Hardie Rawnsley made a tour of Trust properties in Wales and the west of England, descriptions of which were later published in his book *A Nation's Heritage* (1920). The open spaces of course received the most attention, with long descriptions of their beauty and their historical associations. For Hardie, prehistory, the mystery of long barrows and tumuli, silent testimony to lost civilisations, held the greatest attraction, especially if overgrown with a rich and blossoming flora, as they were on the Holnicote Estate:

> Upward we went towards the open moorland, saw the
> memorial hut in which Lady Acland delights to enjoy the

mountain air, and above it the Bury Castle or earthwork of the aboriginal British times. Away at the head of the Combe, still black from the fire that took place there last year, we saw such a sight of foxglove multitude as we had never before beheld. The grass had been burnt here, and the result of the fire was this magnificent display of foxglove beauty. We went on through fern and heather till we reached the upper down, covered with broom and fescue-grass that shimmered in the wind. Tough feeding this, and only the older sheep can tackle it. Gulls wheeled overhead, and higher still we went northward towards the sea.[21]

Further on, during his visit to Morte Point, Hardie, who was not beyond inventing history, delights to give the precise location of a 'cromlech' of which, in his own words,

guide book writers and local historians seem blissfully ignorant . . . It is impossible to say by what power this huge stone was ever placed in position. It may surmount the little burial cairn in which some British or Viking chieftain was once buried, probably in a sitting posture; but it is possible that the whole structure was once covered with earth, which centuries of storm have washed away, and the large stone which closed the burial cairn has long been dragged out of place and lies hard by. I said British or Viking, but remembering the home of the Norseman, and that this cromlech looks due north, it is not impossible that this records a Northern chieftain's place of sepulture. It is certainly one of the most interesting prehistoric monuments in North Devon, if it is a cromlech.[22]

The history of Barrington Court, an Elizabethan manor house near Ilminster which was the Trust's only large country house at that time, is treated somewhat less extensively. His enthusiasm for the building, however, is evident from the full description given of the external features and the interior.

We saw at once, as was fitting in the time of Elizabeth, that the house had been built in the form of the letter E. The angle buttresses of the wings and porch rose up to twisted terminals. These ended in cupola-like tops. The gable ends were finished with like terminals, and all the chimneys were

twisted and gave great lightness and attraction to the
building. Light and grace were its marked features ... We
noticed as we went through the house the enormous
amount of space used for passages, and the comparatively
small number of living-rooms. A good insight into
Elizabethan ways was gained by our visit to the huge open
garrets, with little recesses for cubicles to accommodate the
servants, which ran from end to end of the house. We were
not astonished to hear that at one time five hundred
Parliamentary soldiers were accommodated in this attic.
The only creatures accommodated there now are the owls, and
though the windows have been built up to prevent their
easy entrance, they still find their way thither, and as our
hostess told us, make a noise at night as if people were
shuffling about and dragging weights over the rough
boarding.[23]

Sadly, much of the interior had been gutted. The Trust's tenant in
Hardie's time was a member of the family which had farmed the
estate for a century. The large orchards which stretched away from
one end of the house reminded Hardie that

one of the chief assets of the tenant is the possibility of
cider-making. How good that cider was we were soon to
know, for Mr Jacobs, with true yeoman courtesy, sent out
to beg us rest in the front porch, and with the message
also sent a jug of his own excellent liquor.[24]

Barrington Court today houses showrooms for a firm making
reproduction period English oak interiors and furniture.

The purchase of Barrington Court was made possible in 1907 by
the generosity of Miss J. L. Woodward, who wished to see the
house preserved. In the same year, the National Trust Act reached
the Statute Book. Drafted by Robert Hunter, it conferred on the
Trust the power to declare property inalienable: land or buildings
'cannot be compulsorily acquired by Government departments,
local authorities or any other agency without special parliamentary procedure'. The majority of Trust holdings are protected in
this way, thus providing an assurance to donors that their gifts in
future will be safeguarded. The decision of the Trust Council in
1982, however, taken at first without reference to the membership,
to lease land at Bradenham in Buckinghamshire to the Ministry of
Defence for the construction of a NATO command bunker, dented

public confidence in the concept of inalienability. For its time, the 1907 Act was undoubtedly the most effective legislation that could have been drafted; it was a further 30 years before the Trust required additional legislative powers.

Two of the Trust's founders died before the outbreak of the First World War: in many ways their passing marked the end of an era. The death of Octavia Hill in 1912 was an occasion of national mourning. Apart from Florence Nightingale, no other woman had been so respected as a social reformer in her own lifetime. A burial in Westminster Abbey was offered, but she had left instructions that she wished to be interred in the churchyard at Crockham in Kent, near the cottage she had shared with Harriot Yorke. The funeral, witnessed only by family and close friends, including Bob Hunter, took place as Hardie Rawnsley delivered the eulogy at her memorial service in Southwark Cathedral.

The reasons why Octavia Hill's name is no longer well known were becoming apparent towards the end of her life. She had placed great faith in the power of voluntary agencies and social case-work, both of which had proved only marginally effective in relieving urban poverty. As a result of systematic social surveys of poverty, public opinion was now changing to an awareness of the need for state pensions and welfare services. When she was appointed to the Royal Commission on the Poor Laws in 1905, the gulf between her views and those of some of the other commissioners was clearly evident; she appeared to Beatrice Webb and the Fabians to be obsessed with the self-help philosophy of a bygone age. Octavia's opponents were not unjustified in charging her with patronising the poor, rather than conceding them equal rights. Because she considered that politics was 'man's work' she was not in favour of votes for women, and the suffragettes were furious that such a prominent woman should express this view in public.

The hostility shown by Octavia Hill's opponents because of her unfashionable attitudes did not cause her excessive concern. She had achieved almost all her objectives when in the Spring of 1912, she contracted lung cancer, a tragic irony for one who had spearheaded a campaign for clean air. Handing over to her successors in charity work the nine separate bank accounts for which she was responsible, Octavia set out for one last holiday with Harriot Yorke. They went no further than Larksfield, the cottage where they were accustomed to spend most weekends during the summer. They stayed for several weeks, returning to Marylebone in June. Octavia died at home on the night of 13 August 1912. Hydon Heath, south of Godalming, was purchased in her memory by public subscription and given to the National Trust in 1915.

Sam Hamer, who was secretary of the Trust from 1911–33, was the source of many reminiscences of Octavia, and of strenuous weekends at Larksfield. Guests were likely to be set to digging up docks and thistles, or removing huge flints from the flowerbeds in the afternoons, the morning having been spent asserting rights of way on behalf of the Kent and Surrey branch of the CPS. Given the option one Sunday morning of church or country walk, Hamer recalled to Octavia's biographer W. T. Hill that he rashly elected for the walk. This turned out to be rather more than he bargained for. The exact route was prescribed, across a private estate, and his duty was

> to follow the footpath rigorously, *wherever it led*. 'What if the path goes by the landowner's front windows?'
> 'Oh, that's just what it does!' exclaimed Octavia with her invincible smile. 'That's why we want you to go, because it's a right of way and must be kept open.'[25]

On 6 November 1913 Sir Robert Hunter died suddenly of toxaemia at his home in Haslemere. He had continued his indefatigable work as Solicitor to the Post Office until he was taken ill, two weeks before his death. Valued for his diligence, clear sight and fair-mindedness, he had been maintained at his post to direct the long and complex negotiations for the government purchase of the National Telephone Company system from Marconi. Having successfully completed this contract, with an estimated saving of eight million pounds to the taxpayer, his retirement was imminent.

Bob Hunter was buried in the churchyard of St Bartholomew, the parish church of Haslemere. His funeral was attended by a large and distinguished gathering including representatives of the National Trust, the Kyrle Society and the Liberal Party; James Bryce and Shaw-Lefevre on behalf of the CPS and several architects with whom he had been associated in the preservation of historic buildings were also present. A memorial service was held at Christchurch, Newgate Street, near the Post Office headquarters in the City. Consonant with the genuine modesty of his nature, Bob Hunter was buried in an unmarked grave, and no blue plaque records his birthplace in Addington Square.

Hardie Rawnsley, the antithesis of Bob Hunter in nearly every respect, wrote a brief appreciation of his life for the *Cornhill Maga-*

zine early in 1914, which remains to this day, as a reprinted pamphlet, the only published biography of 'a great-hearted Christian gentleman'.

> He was perfectly fearless, even in dealing with friends, when he thought their action was likely to interfere with the beauty of natural scenery, and the Haslemere people will not soon forget the speech he made in protest against the enlargement of the Parish Church at Haslemere, on the ground that to alter it would destroy its character and its harmony with the quiet village surroundings. He loved that Parish Church dearly and was a devout and constant worshipper there. His body rests beneath its shadow, but his soul will live and move among the people, and be a constant source of inspiration to public spirit and unselfish zeal.[26]

Fourteen acres at Waggoners Wells, a string of hammer-ponds forming one of the sources of the River Wey, was given to the National Trust in 1919, and dedicated to his memory.

The National Trust might have lost Hardie Rawnsley only four years after its foundation, when he was offered the Bishopric of Madagascar. After much heart-searching, and a letter from Octavia Hill pleading with him to stay, he decided that he could not leave his beloved northern fells. Two years before the outbreak of the First World War, however, he did accept an Honorary Chaplaincy to King George V.

As far back as 1897, a note of impending doom is sounded in Hardie's article on the National Trust in the *Cornhill Magazine*, where he wrote of

> ... the feeling that it is good to have a country to live for as well as a fatherland to die for. There are scattered up and down the land ... men who know not to what great issue the trumpet of another century may call their native land – men who rightly or wrongly believe that when the call comes it will be easier to fight and to die for, as it is easier to work and live for –
> 'This other Eden, demi-Paradise, ...'[27]

Octavia Hill had looked upon military training as an essential part of social improvement, turning boys into men. She was responsible for the foundation of the 1st (London) Cadet Battalion 'The Queen's' Royal Regiment, in Red Cross Hall in Southwark. By 1909 more than 8,000 boys had passed through the Battalion's ranks, many of whom later lost their lives on the fields of Flanders.

Hardie, like most of his generation, had few qualms about the rightness of the call to arms. In 1914 he watched with pride as the young men of Keswick, including his own son, enlisted and marched to the railway station, most of them never to return. He published poems praising the deeds of war heroes. In the Michaelmas service at Crosthwaite he spoke of 'the deep inner meaning of this Armageddon, allowed, as I believe, for a great and wonderful purpose'. Preaching the Founder's Day sermon in Uppingham School Chapel in June 1916, he took as his theme 'the Altar of Sacrifice'. At that time, of 1,760 old boys who had gone to the Front, 127 had already been killed, and 230 wounded or taken prisoner.

And why have the gallant one thousand seven hundred
adventured their lives into death? I answer – because they
were Uppingham boys. As I look out on that sea of blood
that is being so willingly poured out by foe and friend
alike, I cannot help being struck with the enthusiasm with
which both sides in this terrible mile on mile of battle offer
themselves a sacrifice for their fellow men and a great ideal.[28]

As time went on, and the lengthening casualty lists from the Battle of the Somme swelled the sacrifice, confidence in the 'great ideal' was shaken and this last sentence was deleted from the revised version of the sermon which Hardie preached in Carlisle Cathedral.

In the winter of 1916, during his three-months' residency as a Cathedral Canon, Hardie was recovering from an attack of influenza when his wife was taken seriously ill. On New Year's eve he received news of her death, and a few days later was still too weak to attend her funeral.

Left without Edith's help and companionship, he decided to retire completely from the ministry at Crosthwaite. After a valedictory service and a farewell party with his parishioners, he closed the door on the Vicarage for the last time. His new home was to be Allan Bank, the house at Grasmere which was once the home of Wordsworth. He had bought Allan Bank with Edith for his retirement and was to bequeath it to the National Trust. Here, with the secretarial assistance of Eleanor Simpson, author of the Grasmere

Plays, who had been a friend for many years, Hardie set his mind purposefully to the work of helping to keep the Trust going through the wartime stringency which reduced its income.

Within 18 months of Edith's death Hardie caused a minor scandal by his apparently sudden second marriage to Eleanor, who was much younger than himself. His tour of the National Trust properties in the West of England that summer was their honeymoon, Hardie dictating his last book to her as they went along.

In whatever activity he was engaged, Hardie Rawnsley's zeal continued unabated. In 1919 Hardie was organising the national distribution of fireworks for the peace celebrations. He remained fully involved in diocesan committee work. Deeply concerned about the effects of pornography, he served on a committee to combat the spread of 'pernicious literature' and rude postcards. Health, in the broadest sense, had always been his interest, and he had assisted in the foundation of a sanatorium, not far from Keswick, for the treatment of tuberculosis. He also risked a lawsuit on one occasion by issuing a pamphlet attacking the milling industry for its use of steel rollers to remove the roughage from wheat. News that the National Trust now produces stone-ground flour at Dunster Mill in Somerset would have sent him into raptures, and no doubt occasioned several celebratory sonnets.

At a meeting of Convocation in York in the Spring of 1920, Hardie suffered a severe heart attack. He insisted on fulfilling a preaching engagement four days later, and when he eventually arrived home at Allan Bank, he continued to conduct business as usual from his bed. In the weeks before his death, Eleanor records how from his bedroom window Hardie watched the cherry tree blossom and fade, and a great copper beech burst into bud and leaf.

> He eagerly listened for the notes of the various migrants,
> waiting with daily expectation for the coming of the pied
> fly-catcher, and when at last he caught sight of its 'domino
> dress' welcomed its arrival with a poem.[29]

He died on 28 May, and was buried in Crosthwaite churchyard next to his first wife. A memorial service was held in Carlisle Cathedral, where there is now a plaque bearing his portrait in the south Quire aisle. Friars Crag, Lords Island and a part of Great Wood on Derwent Water were given to the National Trust in his memory 'by subscribers who wish that his name shall not be forgotten'. *The Times* observed that 'England would be a much duller and less happy and healthy country if he had not lived and worked'.[30]

Of all the founders of the National Trust, Hardie Rawnsley was the most dynamic embodiment of the campaigning spirit which once characterised that organisation. It was a spirit shared by all three, who, as the early reports of the Trust Council show, were concerned about the fate of beautiful landscape or buildings of historical merit irrespective of whether or not they were destined for the Trust. Robert Hunter had been one of the principals in the preservation of several of London's most interesting old buildings, including Charterhouse, Staple Inn, the French Almshouses in Mile End Road and the Ironmongers' Almshouse in the Kingsland Road, although the Trust did not in fact acquire any of these.

Shortly after its foundation, the National Trust was making vociferous protests against the British Aluminium Company's scheme to harness the Falls of Foyers on the banks of Loch Ness for a hydroelectric scheme. The 1896 Report says that 'the Society exceedingly regrets that its opposition to this piece of vandalism proved unavailing, and the Falls are now to all intents and purposes destroyed'. The executive went on to oppose hydroelectric power schemes elsewhere, with more success, and also managed to put an end to quarrying in the Cheddar Gorge. In her book *Back to the Land* (1982) Jan Marsh notes that the Trust 'prevented the construction of at least two railway lines, at Henley and Lynmouth'.[31]

In the Lake District, the Trust from the outset was seen as an organisation entirely in sympathy with the aims and objects of the Lake District Defence Society. The acquisition of land in the Lakes was secondary to the cardinal principle of preserving the character of the entire region. Hardie campaigned to prevent the erection of overhead electric cables, insensitive road schemes, hydroplanes on the lakes and the felling of natural oak woods to make way for the planting of fir trees. His concern for vernacular architecture is well illustrated in his long and tireless struggle to save the beautiful ancient bridge which spanned the River Derwent at Portinscale. The highway authority wanted it dismantled to allow for a wider road, and on several occasions from 1907 onwards, the demolition order came perilously close to being put into effect. The National Trust, in collaboration with the RAC, issued a statement declaring that 'in a neighbourhood like the Lake District to which motorists go to enjoy the scenery, the last thing they desire is that roads should be straightened and picturesque bridges interfered with'.

After heated arguments and negotiations lasting seven years, the Portinscale Bridge was finally saved and restored. Unfortunately, it did not, as the writer of a parody of Macaulay hoped, last until the year 'AD 2000' when

> ... With weeping and with laughter
> Still is the story told
> How Hardie Rawnsley held the Bridge
> In the brave days of old.[32]

None the less, it continued to carry all the necessary traffic until damaged beyond repair by severe flooding in the 1950s. The River Derwent is now spanned by the featureless three-lane highway built in the mid-1970s, despite the Latrigg protest.

The Trust's campaigning spirit, it appears, began to decline once the pioneering influence of the founders was lost.[33]

The Council for the Preservation of Rural England, founded in 1926, took up many of the causes which had once been the National Trust's concern, not just in the Lake District, but throughout Britain.

The Trust now tends to see its brief concerning the countryside as mainly restricted to its own properties, although many issues remain part of a much wider debate. For example, the campaign to prevent the construction of a bypass on Trust land at Petworth Park in 1975 was one in a long series of protests which occurred in areas of exceptional beauty. Recently the Trust has adopted a number of 'sustainable' practices in agriculture and horticulture. A ban on the use of certain insecticides is written into the tenancy agreements of many of the 700-odd National Trust farms. The Trust is also committed to a soil restoration programme and is rapidly phasing out the use of peat-based composts in its gardens. However, admirable though these practices may be, the organisation is responding to the concerns of the wider ecological community rather than being in the vanguard of reform.

It is for the historians of a later period of the Trust's development to consider whether the campaigning spirit of the founders has lost some of its momentum. Enterprise Neptune, the appeal for the coastline, has been cited as epitomising the spirit of campaign in the present day. This was certainly true at the time of its launch in 1965 by Conrad Rawnsley, Hardie's grandson, who was its architect, and for the first eighteen months its director. It took just 19 years to add 263 miles to the 187 miles of unspoilt coastline already in Trust ownership, thereby achieving half the appeal's target. Since Neptune's re-launch in 1985 a further 125 miles has been added to the total, including six miles of the Durham coast, where the beaches have been cleared of waste tips and restored to their original condition.

In the acquisition of open spaces in general, the Trust policy has been fairly consistent with the intentions of its founders. By 2001 it had achieved ownership of 612,000 acres in England, Wales and Northern Ireland, including more than a quarter of the Lake District National Park. It continues to be the case that the great majority of Trust properties, land and buildings, are in those areas where the founders made acquisitions in the early years, and are generally in those parts of the country most at risk from pressure of population and tourism. Unfortunately, apart from the Lake District, the concentration of properties in the South of England accentuates the great divide between north and south, reflected in so many institutions in British society. There has been an effort in recent years to correct this imbalance, notably the appeal which attracted £4½ million for the purchase of 4,000 acres of land in Snowdonia.

Since the mid 1960s the pace of the Trust's acquisition of land has slowed down, and in most people's minds today, it is an organisation associated first and foremost with the preservation of stately homes, and only secondly with open spaces and the coastline. This association in the public mind with grand houses came about as the result of the conscious change of direction in policy which took place in the mid 1930s. The passing of a new National Trust Act in 1937 facilitated the acquisition of large country houses by allowing land or investments to be held in order to provide an income for their upkeep. Public interest in visiting stately homes, their gardens and deer parks, has been aroused in recent years by costume drama, popular history and gardening programmes on television.

National Trust membership now stands at over two-and-three-quarter million, having at the time of writing (2002) quadrupled over twenty-five years; this continuing rise is an indication of the enormous popularity of the Trust's great country houses, to which members are admitted free of charge. Wherever possible the Trust's policy is to preserve the houses and their contents as an entity, and to avoid the dispersal of collections of fine art, furniture and porcelain accumulated by the original owners. The donors and their descendants are encouraged to remain in occupation as tenants in order to retain the family connection with the property.

Since the institution of the Country Houses Scheme, concentration of resources on stately homes has inevitably been at the expense of other types of building such as tithe barns, artisans' dwellings and houses of the lesser landed gentry.[34] The National Trust still cares for too few urban buildings, particularly outside London.[35] Archaeological as well as aesthetic and historical criteria play an increasing role in decision-making over acquisitions. Cotehele in Cornwall and Chastleton in Oxfordshire are amongst those houses particularly prized as unchanged 'time-capsules' – both remaining in the exterior and interior condition of the period during which they were constructed and furnished, with few later accretions. Recently however, the founders' enthusiasm for buildings of a modest nature has been rediscovered. The Trust has surveyed its thousands of smaller buildings, the majority of which are tenanted farms and cottages not open to the public, and has begun the process of acquiring both representative and unusual examples of houses in the urban environment. Town houses opened fairly recently comprise an Edwardian semi-detached house, a Victorian gentleman's villa, a council house and a Modernist terrace. Trust buildings acquired during the lifetime of the founders, though few, represented a less grandiose but more balanced microcosm of social history and family life than is the case today, with almost 200 houses and castles open to the public. Two of the Trust's latest purchases, however, a nineteenth-century workhouse at Southwell in Nottinghamshire and a block of back-to-back houses in Birmingham, show there is a willingness to cast a wider net in the search for buildings of historic interest.

The agricultural revolution which has taken place since the Second World War, resulting in intensive pressure on farmland, has wrought drastic changes in the English countryside. Old-established field patterns have been lost as hedgerows have been uprooted, ponds and wetlands drained, downland ploughed and deciduous woodland replaced by ugly and monotonous conifer plantations. The National Trust has been able to resist this pressure on its own land, and has played an important part in conserving the traditional appearance of some of the most beautiful English landscape. It insists on farming methods consonant with good husbandry, and does not permit the degradation of its land for quick profit. Undoubtedly the founders would have approved if the organisation had campaigned in recent years for an extension of these policies beyond its own properties, or sought to acquire and protect a wider range of wildlife habitats such as 'raised mires, water meadows, hay meadows, unimproved grassland, chalk and limestone river systems, ancient lime and hazel woods and old orchards.' More attention to these features would increase the Trust's holdings beyond the areas in which the founders lived, and

extend its interest into open countryside currently under-repre-
sented: the Midlands, eastern and north-east England, mid- and
South Wales.[36]

The ideal of voluntary service to the community, which motivated the founders, is still an essential feature of the National
Trust's organisation. Volunteer guides and wardens play an
important part in the day-to-day management of the properties.

Young volunteers carry out numerous conservation and rehabil-
itation projects, acquiring skills which may later equip them for
full-time employment. The continuing success of the Trust owes
much to these unpaid helpers, to whom the broad philosophy of
the founders must be important if their altruism is to be well
directed. The policy of actively recruiting volunteers from all
sections of society, including young people from the inner cities, is
a logical extension of that philosophy.

The purpose of this book has been to give an account of the
founders' intentions. They were united in their deeply felt
concerns: to improve the quality of life for people living in cities,
and to satisfy the common human need for fresh air and open
space.

The tendency to promote Octavia Hill as the moving spirit and
principal instigator of the National Trust would seem to date from
the inception of the Country Houses Scheme, which harks back to
the idea she put forward at the inaugural meeting in 1894. Sir
Sydney Cockerell wrote in *The Times* of 28 February 1935, on the
fortieth anniversary of the Trust's legal incorporation: 'Of those
who called the National Trust into being in 1895 Octavia Hill occu-
pies the central place, with Canon Rawnsley and Sir Robert Hunter
on either side.'

This is a distorted view of history, and from the evidence here
presented it must be obvious that the National Trust could not
have been conceived without the vision and energy contributed to
its development equally by all three founders.

Appendix

LAY OF MODERN ENGLAND

AUGUSTUS SMITH, of Scilly,
  By Piper's Hole he swore
That the proud Lord of Brownlow
  Should keep the waste no more.
By Piper's Hole he swore it,
  And named a trysting night,
And bade his myrmidons ride forth,
By special train from London's north,
  To venge the Common Right.

Where on the street of Drummond
  Four Doric columns frown,
Where the gigantic STEPHENSON
  On his own line looks down,
The stalwart navvies gathered,
  From lodgings far and near;
Strong were the crowbars in their hands,
  Stronger their hope for beer.

Loured the foul London gaslights;
  And made the gloom more deep,
The million-peopled city's sons
  Were in their early sleep,
When from the Euston Station
  Glided the special train
That bore the force that went to win
  Berkhampstead's waste again.

And sternly rode each navvy,
  The crowbar in his gripe,
And scornful of the snob-made law,
  A fire in every pipe;
They rode in solemn silence,
  And not a navvy knew,
The leader whom he went to serve,
  The work he went to do.

Thine old Red Cap, O Mother!
  That train went rushing by,
Where Willesden bears JACK SHEPPARD's

              name
  In holiest memory.
Where points to Heaven the spire
  On Harrow's haunted Hill,
Where Pinner's perky stockbrokers
  In cockney nests were still.

Through Bushey and through Watford,
  And on to wild Boxmoor
That special train its weighty freight
  Of rugged champions bore.
On, the steam-demon bore them,
  Nor flagged upon the wing,
Until he lighted with his load
  At Baptist-chapelled Tring.

Then spoke a voice accustomed
  To bid strong men obey:
I know full well whose voice it was:
  His name I may not say.
"This way," was all He uttered,
  As brief was their reply,
The navvy wastes few idle words–
  The navvies grunted "Ay."

They marched three miles in silence,
  The road was dark and drear,
But thought upheld the navvy's heart:
  The pleasant thought of beer.
They reached Berkhampstead Common,
  Or that which had been one,
Until by Ashridge's proud Lord
  The feudal deed was done.

There, miles of iron railing
  Scowled grimly in the dark
Making what once was Common,
  The Lord of Brownlow's Park:
His rights that Lord asserted,
  Rights which they hold a myth,

The bold Berkhampstead Commoners,
   Led by AUGUSTUS SMITH.

Spoke out the nameless Leader,
   "That Railing must go down."
Then firmer grasped the crowbar
   Those hands so strong and brown,
They march against the railing,
   They lay the crowbars low,
And down and down for many a yard
   The costly railings go.

Strong are the navvies' muscles,
   The navvies work like men:
Where was the Lord of Brownlow,
   Where was brave PAXTON then?
Where was the valiant GROVER,
   The gallant STOCKEN where,
And where was he who smokes the
      hams,
   And makes the Earl his care?

Yes, where was grocer HAZELL,
   Who raised the duteous song:
"As how a Lord like Brownlow's Lord
   Could never do what's wrong?"
The Earl and all his champions
   Were sleeping far away
And ere the morn, upon the gorse
   Three miles of railing lay.

"Hurrah!" the navvies shouted:
   In sight a horseman glides:
See on his cob, with bob, bob, bob,
   The duteous HAZELL rides:
To do his Lordship service
   Comes riding through the mirk,
And bids the navvies let him know
   Who brought them to their work.

Answer the stalwart navvies,
   Who smoke the ham-smoker's game,
"Behold'st" thou, HAZELL, yon canal;
   Would'st like to swim the same?
If not, with beer this instant
   Thyself and cob redeem,"
And round him as they spoke, they drew,
   And edged him near the stream.

So down went BROWNLOW's railing,
   And down went HAZELL's beer,
And from the gathering crowd upgoes
   One loud and lusty cheer.
For carriage, gig, and dog-cart
   Come rushing on the scene,
And all Berkhampstead hastes to see
   Where BROWNLOW's rails had been.

And husbands, wives, and children,
   Went strolling through the gorse,
And cried, "We've got our own again,
   Thanks to your friendly force."
They cut green little morsels
   As memories of the Band,
Whose lusty arms and iron bars
   Had freed the Common land.

Bold was the deed and English
   The Commoners have done,
Let's hope the law of England, too,
   Will smile upon their fun.
For our few remaining Commons
   Must not be seized or sold,
Nor Lords forget they do not live
   In the bad days of old.

The reclamation of Berkhamsted Common,
Punch, 24 March 1866

Notes

Chapter 1 The Beginning of the Open Space Movement

1. Thomas Hardy, description of Egdon Heath in *The Return of the Native*, Ch.1.

2. W. G. Hoskins and L. Dudley Stamp, *The Common Lands of England and Wales* (Collins, 1963) p.55.

3. Ibid., p.61.

4. E. Robinson and D. Powell (eds.), *John Clare* (OUP, 1984) p.46.

5. Hansard, vol.177, pp.510–14.

6. Ibid., vol. 182, p.368.

7. 'Memorandum on the foundation of the Commons Preservation Society' 1868, Guildhall Library fo.pam. 123.

8. Hugh Elliot (ed.), *Letters of John Stuart Mill* (Longmans, Green, 1910) vol.2, pp.56–7.

9. *The Times*, 23 Jan. 1866.

10. Ibid., 25 Jan. 1866.

11. G. H. Whybrow, *The History of Berkhamsted Common* (CPS, c.1930) p.48.

12. Ibid., pp.145–6.

13. Ibid., pp.80–3.

14. Lord Eversley, *Commons, Forests and Footpaths* (Cassell, 1910) p.46.

15. *Punch*, 24 Mar. 1866, vol.50, p.125.

16. Whybrow, *Berkhamsted Common*, pp.90–2.

17. Eversley, *Commons*, pp.30–1, 47–53.

18. Ibid., pp.55–9.

19. 'A Glance at the Commons and Open Spaces near London', Guildhall Library fo.pam.5709.

20. Eversley, *Commons*, p.32.

Chapter 2 Robert Hunter

1. Most of the information about Bob Hunter's childhood is from Ann Hunter, 'Reminiscences and some anecdotes told me by my Mother or Aunt Sarah Anne' and 'Early Personal Notes and Work', undated, unpublished MSS.

2. *Six Essays on Commons Preservation* (Sampson Low, Son and Marston, 1867) p.368.

3. Eversley, *Commons*, p.59.

4. Ibid., pp.59–72.

5. Leslie Stephen, *Life of Henry Fawcett* (Smith, Elder, 1886) p.294.

6. Ibid., p.62.

7. Ibid., p.302.

8. Alfred Qvist, *Epping Forest* (The Sidney Press, Bedford, 1971).

9. John Manwood, *A Treatise of the Laws of the Foreſt* (3rd edn) (Company of Stationers, 1665) pp.40–1.

10. Hansard, vol.175, p.1207.

11. Percy Thompson, 'The Willingales of Loughton: to whom do we owe Epping Forest?', *Essex Naturalist*, vol.21, pp.157–69.

12. 'Memorial to the Right Hon. A. H. Layard, M.P.' Guildhall Library fo.pam.2028(i).

13. Stephen, *Henry Fawcett*, pp.313–14.

14. Dorothy Hunter, 'The Epping Forest Case', undated, unpublished MS, p.6.

15. Eversley, *Commons*, p.98.

16. Stephen, *Henry Fawcett*, p.320.

17. *Daily Telegraph*, 30 June 1874.

18. Dorothy Hunter, 'The Epping Forest Case', pp.9–10.

19. Ibid., pp.12–13.

20. *Daily Telegraph*, 1 July 1874.

21. Ibid., 11 Nov. 1874.

22. Eversley, *Commons*, p.110.

23. Ibid., p.108.

24. *The Times*, 8 May 1882.

25. C. J. Cornish, *The New Forest* (Commin, 1899) p.73.

26. *The Times*, 7 Nov. 1913.

27. Ibid.

Chapter 3 Octavia Hill

1. E. Moberly Bell, *Octavia Hill, a Biography* (Constable, 1942) p.5.

2. Ibid., p.10.

3. Ibid., p.29.

4. C. E. Maurice, *Life of Octavia Hill as told in her Letters* (Macmillan, 1913) p.38.

5. E. S. Maurice, *Octavia Hill, Early Ideals* (Allen & Unwin, 1928) pp.129–31.

6. Octavia Hill, 'Organized Work among the Poor', *Macmillan's Magazine* (July 1869) vol.20, p.220.

7. E. S. Maurice, *Early Ideals*, p.199.

8. Octavia Hill, *Our Common Land* (Macmillan, 1877) pp.166–7.

9. E. S. Maurice, *Early Ideals*, p.90.

10. Ibid., pp.186–7.

11. See Stephen, *Henry Fawcett*, p.328.

12. Hansard, vol.227, p.543.

13. *Report of the C.P.S.* 1870–1876, 2nd edn (1877) p.33. The record of the Home Secretary's speech here conflicts with Hansard, so the epigram is quoted from what appears to be its earliest printed source: *The Tickler Magazine*, 1 Feb. 1821.

14. Octavia Hill, 'Our Common Land', *Macmillan's Magazine* (April 1876) vol.33, pp.538–9.

15. Stephen, *Henry Fawcett*, p.332.

16. Ibid.

17. R. Hunter, 'The Movements for the Inclosure and Preservation of Open Lands', *Journal of the Royal Statistical Society* (June 1897) vol.60, p.395.

18. Bell, *Octavia Hill*, p.163.

19. Octavia Hill, 'Space for the People', *Macmillan's Magazine* (Aug. 1875) vol.32, p.328.

20. Octavia Hill, *Our Common Land*, p.151.

21. Evidence to the 'Select Committee on Public Walks' 1833 – 'Leaving the Regent's Park towards the East, Your Committee regret to state that for several miles along the Northern edge of the Metropolis, all the way to the River at Limehouse, there is not a single place reserved as a Park or Public Walk, planted and laid out for the accommodation of the People; yet there is no part of London where such Improvements are more imperatively called for.' *British Sessional Papers*, vol.15, p.337.

22. Octavia Hill, *Our Common Land*, p.107 et seq.

23. Ibid., pp.116–17.

24. Ibid., pp.121–2.

25. Ibid., pp.119–20.

26. 44/45 Vict. c.34, s.3.

27. Eversley, *Commons*, p.188.

28. Ibid.

29. C. E. Maurice, *Life of Octavia Hill*, pp.387–8 (emphasis in the original).

30. Quoted in J. D. Rosenberg, *The Darkening Glass* (Columbia UP 1961) pp.212–14.

31. 'Fourth Annual Report by the Inspector' under the Alkali Act 1863 (Eyre & Spottiswoode, 1868) pp.56–60.

32. 38/9 Vict., c.55, s.91.

33. Bell, *Octavia Hill*, p.168.

34. Letter from Octavia Hill and Robert Hunter, *The Times*, 19 Dec. 1885.

35. *The Times*, 3 Nov. 1884.

Chapter 4 Hardwicke Rawnsley

1. G. Berry and G. Beard, *The Lake District: A Century of Conservation* (John Bartholomew, 1980) pp.41–8.

2. Quoted in J. D. Marshall and J. K. Walton, *The Lake Counties from 1830 to mid-Twentieth Century* (Manchester UP, 1981) p.208.

3. 'Ode to Shiplake', c.1861, Rawnsley MS C5; E. F. Rawnsley, *Canon Rawnsley: an Account of his Life* (MacLehose, Jackson, 1923) p.7.

4. H. D. Rawnsley, *Past and Present at the English Lakes* (James MacLehose, 1916) p.260.

5. H. D. Rawnsley, *Memories of the Tennysons* (James MacLehose, 1912) p.58; W. F. Rawnsley, *Highways and Byways in Lincolnshire* (Macmillan, London, 1914) p.314.

6. H. D. Rawnsley, 'Sermon delivered at Church of St Andrew, Halton Holgate on 24 April 1911', Cumbria R.O., Kendal WDX/402.

7. M. Tozer, 'Physical Education at Thring's Uppingham', MEd thesis, University of Leicester 1974; see H. D. Rawnsley, *Edward Thring as Teacher and Poet* (Fisher Unwin, 1889).

8. E. F. Rawnsley, *Canon Rawnsley*, p.12.

9. Ibid., p.14.

10. Ibid., pp.24–5.

11. H. D. Rawnsley, 'The Power of Personal Service – A Sermon in Memory of Octavia Hill, preached in Southwark Cathedral, 21 August 1912', Cumbria R.O., WDX/402, p.10; by his Sons, *Robert Somervell* (Faber & Faber, 1935) pp.59–62.

12. E. F. Rawnsley, *Canon Rawnsley*, p.33; see F. Borwick (ed.), *Clifton College Annals & Register 1862–1925* (Arrowsmith, 1925) ch.XVI; *The History of St Agnes' Parish* (Arrowsmith, 1890).

13. H. D. Rawnsley, *A Book of Bristol Sonnets* (Hamilton, Adams, 1877) pp.24–5.

14. Testimonial from Inhabitants of the Area served by Clifton College Mission to H. D. Rawnsley, 8 Dec. 1877, Rawnsley MS D8; Letter from H. D. Rawnsley to his mother, 10 Dec. 1877, ibid., C9; Letter from E. Thring to Mrs Drummond Rawnsley, 11 Dec. 1877, ibid., P3.

15. See H. D. Rawnsley, *By Fell and Dale at the English Lakes* (James MacLehose, 1911) pp.27–35.

16. H. D. Rawnsley, *Sonnets at the English Lakes* (Longmans, Green, 1881) p.36.

17. Judy Taylor, *Beatrix Potter, Artist, Storyteller and Country-woman* (Frederick Warne, Penguin, 1986).

18. *Robert Somervell*, pp.50–6.

19. H. D. Rawnsley, *Harvey Goodwin, Bishop of Carlisle* (John Murray, 1896) p.193.

20. E. F. Rawnsley, *Canon Rawnsley*, pp.49–50.

21. Ibid., p.51.

22. H. D. Rawnsley 'The Proposed Permanent Lake District Defence Society', John Rylands Library fo.R5239, pp.7–8.

23. Letter from John Ruskin to H. D. Rawnsley, by courtesy of Mr G. Simpson, Keswick.

24. E. F. Rawnsley, *Canon Rawnsley*, p.53.

25. Ibid., p.52.

26. MS in Carlisle R.O. DSO/24/15/1; see postcard from Octavia Hill to H. D. Rawnsley, 17 Nov. 1885, Carlisle R.O. DSO/24/7/2.

27. E. F. Rawnsley, *Canon Rawnsley*, p.53.

28. Marshall and Walton, *The Lake Counties*, p.214.

29. H. D. Rawnsley, 'The Proposed Permanent Lake District Defence Society', p.12.

30. William Wordsworth 'Introduction' in Joseph Wilkinson, *Select Views in Cumberland, Westmoreland, and Lancashire* (R. Ackerman, 1810) pp.xxxiii–xxxiv.

31. E. F. Rawnsley, *Canon Rawnsley*, p.57.

32. H. D. Rawnsley, *Ruskin and the English Lakes* (James MacLehose, 1901) pp.125–8.

33. Cartoon of Hardie Rawnsley, Rawnsley MS Q; see *West Cumberland Times*, 2 June 1920; H. D. Rawnsley, *Life and Nature at the English Lakes* (James MacLehose, 1902).

34. E. F. Rawnsley, *Canon Rawnsley*, p.161.

35. H. D. Rawnsley, *A Rambler's Notebook at the English Lakes* (James MacLehose, 1902) p.80.

36. *Bird Notes and News, Journal of the R.S.P.B.*, Summer 1920, vol.9, pp.13–14; 'Proceedings of the Annual Meeting, R.S.P.B. 24 Feb. 1904', pp.4–6.

37. H. D. Rawnsley, *A Rambler's Notebook*, pp.13–32.

38. H. D. Rawnsley, 'Footpath Preservation – a National Need', *Contemporary Review*, Sept. 1886, vol.50, p.373.

39. H. D. Rawnsley, *Months at the Lakes* (James MacLehose, 1906) p.51.

40. See H. A. L. Rice, *Lake Country Portraits* (Harvill Press, 1967) p.134; E. F. Rawnsley, *Canon Rawnsley*, pp.244–5.

41. *The English Lakes Visitor and Keswick Guardian*, 15 Oct. 1887.

42. 'Rules of Keswick and District Footpath Association', Carlisle R.O. DSO/24/7/2 and 3; see H. D. Rawnsley, *A Coach Drive at the Lakes: Windermere to Keswick* (T. Bakewell, Keswick, 1891) Association advertisement at the back of this book, pp.95–6.

43. E. F. Rawnsley, *Canon Rawnsley*, p.75; see H. D. Rawnsley, *Lake Country Sketches* (James MacLehose, 1903) p.155.

44. *The English Lakes Visitor*, 3 Sept. and 8 Oct. 1887; see *Manchester Guardian*, 3 and 7 Oct. 1887; *Manchester Weekly Times*, 1 and 8 Oct. 1887.

45. *Isle of Man Examiner*, 22 Oct. 1887.

46. *Cumberland News*, 22 Sept. 1951.

47. *West Cumberland Times*, 2 June 1920.

48. H. D. Rawnsley, *Lake Country Sketches*, pp.150–65; W. G. Collingwood, *The Lake Counties* (Frederick Warne, 1932) pp.158–9; H. D. Rawnsley, *Past and Present*, pp.153–208.

Chapter 5 The Birth of the National Trust

1. R. Hunter, 'The Preservation of Places of Interest or Beauty' – Lecture delivered at Manchester University 29 Jan. 1907 (Manchester UP) pp.11–13.

2. J. Ruskin, *The Seven Lamps of Architecture* (1849) in *Collected Works*, vol.8 (George Allen, 1903) pp.242–4.

3. 'A School of Rational Builders' – Catalogue to an exhibition at the British Architectural Library, 10 March–1 May 1982 (SPAB, 1982).

4. Letter from Octavia Hill to R. Hunter, 22 Aug. 1884, Surrey R.O., Guildford 1260/4/10.

5. *Transactions of the National Association for the Promotion of Social Science*, 17–24 Sept. 1884 (Longmans, Green, 1885) p.754.

6. W. T. Hill, *Octavia Hill, Pioneer of the National Trust and Housing Reformer* (Hutchinson, 1956) pp.145–6.

7. F. M. L. Thompson, *Hampstead: Building a Borough, 1650–1964* (Routledge & Kegan Paul, 1974) pp.330–4.

8. Octavia Hill, 'Natural Beauty as a National Asset', *Nineteenth Century and After*, Dec. 1905, vol.58, p.935.

9. Robin Fedden, *The National Trust, Past and Present* (Jonathan Cape, 1974) p.33.

10. *The Times*, 17 July 1894.

11. See M. Spense (ed.), *Dearest Mama Talbot – A Selection of Letters Written by John Ruskin to Mrs Fanny Talbot* (Allen & Unwin, 1966).

12. J. Dixon–Scott, *England Under Trust* (Macmillan, 1937) p.37.

13. 'A School of Rational Builders', pp.15–16.

14. Quoted in J. S. Dearden, *John Ruskin. An Illustrated Life, 1819–1900* (Brantwood Trust, 1981) p.7.

15. B. L. Thompson, *The Lake District and the National Trust* (Titus Wilson, 1946) pp.42–3.

16. C. E. Maurice, *Life of Octavia Hill*, p.553.

17. H. D. Rawnsley, *Round the Lake Country* (James MacLehose, 1909) p.94.

18. *Westmorland Gazette*, 11 August 1906.

19. B. L. Thompson, *The Lake District and the National Trust*, p.43.

20. E. F. Rawnsley, *Canon Rawnsley*, pp.112–13.

21. H. D. Rawnsley, *A Nation's Heritage* (Allen & Unwin, 1920) p.103.

22. Ibid., pp.129–30.

23. Ibid., pp.85–7.

24. Ibid., p.85.

25. W. T. Hill, *Octavia Hill*, p.149.

26. H. D. Rawnsley, 'A National Benefactor – Sir Robert Hunter', *Cornhill Magazine*, Feb. 1914 (reprinted Spottiswoode) p.12.

27. H. D. Rawnsley, 'The National Trust', *Cornhill Magazine*, Feb. 1897, new series vol.2, pp.245–6.

28. H. D. Rawnsley, 'Uppingham School Founders' Day Sermon', June 1916, Cumbria R.O. WDX 402.

29. E. F. Rawnsley, *Canon Rawnsley*, p.263.

30. *The Times*, 29 May 1920.

31. Jan Marsh, *Back to the Land: The Pastoral Impulse in England from 1880–1914* (Quartet, 1982) p.58.

32. *National Trust News*, Autumn 1975, p.19. See H. D. Rawnsley, *Chapters at the English Lakes* (James MacLehose, 1913) pp.168–90.

33. See Fedden, *The National Trust*, p.27.

34. Notable exceptions are the Yeoman Farmer's House at Troutbeck in Cumbria, the 16c Labourer's Cottage at Hambledon in Surrey, the Fen Cottage at Wicken in Cambridgeshire and, more recently acquired, a Chartist Land Movement Cottage at Dodford in Worcestershire.

35. Progress has been made since the 1960s in opening some well-preserved monuments of the industrial age; among them working examples of a Georgian cotton mill, a tin mine engine and, in Northern Ireland, a beetling mill, a spade manufactory and a fine Victorian pub.

36. Philip Lowe, 'The Countryside', in Howard Newby (ed.), *The National Trust, The Next Hundred Years* (National Trust, 1995) pp.95–6.

Further Reading

Bremner, Douglas, *For the Benefit of the Nation, The National Trust for Scotland: the first 70 years* (National Trust for Scotland, Edinburgh, 2001)

Darley, Gillian, *Octavia Hill* (Constable, London, 1990)

Eversley, Lord, *Commons, Forests and Footpaths* (Cassell, London, 1910)

Gaze, John, *Figures in a Landscape* (Barrie and Jenkins in association with the National Trust, London, 1988)

Hilton, Tim, *John Ruskin*, 2 vols. (Yale UP, 1985, 2000)

Marsh, Jan, *Back to the Land: The Pastoral Impulse in England from 1880–1914* (Quartet, London, 1982)

Marshall, J. D. and Walton, J. K., *The Lake Counties from 1830 to mid-Twentieth Century* (Manchester UP, 1981)

Newby, Howard (ed.), *The National Trust, The Next Hundred Years* (National Trust, London, 1995)

Rawnsley, E. F., *Canon Rawnsley: an Account of his Life* (MacLehose, Jackson, Glasgow, 1923)

Rawnsley, H. D., *A National Benefactor – Sir Robert Hunter* (Spottiswoode, London, 1914)

Waterson, Merlin, *The National Trust: The First Hundred Years* (BBC in association with the National Trust, London, 1994)

Weideger, Paula, *Gilding the Acorn, Behind the Façade of the National Trust* (Simon & Schuster, London, 1994)

Index